Pasta Menus

Great Meals in Minutes was created by Rebus Inc., and published by Time-Life Books.

This edition published 1995 by Bloomsbury Books, an imprint of The Godfrey Cave Group, 42 Bloomsbury Street, London, WC1B 3QJ.

© 1995 Time-Life Books BV.

ISBN 1 85471 596 8

Printed and bound in Great Britain.

$$\boxed{\textit{Great Meals in Minutes}}$$

Pasta Menus

Helen Witty
Menu 1
Hot Sweet-and-Sour Curly Noodle and Ham Salad   8
Courgette Strips Vinaigrette

Menu 2
Spaghettini in Cream with Red Caviar   9
Escarole and Mushroom Salad

Menu 3
An Abundant Antipasto   10
Baked Orzo with Peppers and Cheese

Alfredo Viazzi
Menu 1
Spaghettini with Sausage and Courgettes   14
String Bean Salad with Nuts and Cream

Menu 2
Linguine with Scallops   16
Broccoli Salad

Menu 3
Pasticcio di Lasagnette   18
Arugula Salad

Ed Giobbi
Menu 1
Spaghettini with Salad Greens   22
Veal Chops in Paper Bags
Baked Asparagus

Menu 2
Macaroni Country Style   24
Orange and Olive Salad

Menu 3
Spaghettini Primavera   26
Fillet of Sole with Vegetables
Baked Spinach

Bernice Hunt
Menu 1
Fresh Figs or Melon with Prosciutto   30
Cartwheels with Mixed Vegetables

Menu 2
Carrot Soup   31
Fusilli with Chicken and Rosemary

Menu 3
Mushroom Salad   32
Fettuccine alla Carbonara
Steamed Broccoli with Lemon Juice and Olive Oil

Sylvia Rosenthal
Menu 1
Tortellini Salad   36
Poached Glazed Chicken Breasts

Menu 2
Mushrooms Riviera   37
Baked Macaroni with Ham and Cheese
Tossed Green Salad

Menu 3
Fettuccine with Gorgonzola Sauce   39
Veal Scallopini with Lemon and Parsley
Carrots and Peas with Dill

Diane Darrow and Tom Maresca
Menu 1
Sliced Tomatoes with Tuna Sauce   44
Spaghetti with Peppers, Aubergines, and Tomatoes

Menu 2
Veal Tartare   46
Capelli d'Angelo with Asparagus Sauce

Menu 3
Mozzarella Tart   48
Rigatoni with Mushroom and Chicken Liver Sauce
Spinach and Chicory Salad

Jane Salzfass Freiman
Menu 1
Spaghettini with Yogurt Pesto   54
Grilled Salmon Fillets with Chives in Lemon Butter Sauce
Sliced Tomato and Goat Cheese Salad

Menu 2
Sliced Prosciutto with Country Bread   56
Pasta Salad with Asparagus and Shrimp

Menu 3
Pasta and Mussels with Herbed Tomato-and-
   Garlic Sauce   48
Quick Curry Roasted Chicken
Mushroom, Endive, and Watercress Salad with Vinaigrette

Bloomsbury Books
London

Helen Witty

Menu 1
(*Right*)
Hot Sweet-and-Sour Curly Noodle
and Ham Salad
Courgette Strips Vinaigrette

Helen Witty, who has lived on both coasts, is an admirer of many cuisines, as you will discover when you prepare her recipes. She draws from many cooking traditions to produce unorthodox pasta combinations. Menu 1 and 3, in particular, feature ethnic flavours not usually associated with pasta. The sweet-and-sour pasta salad in Menu 1 is a descendant of the savoury salads that are popular with the Pennsylvania Dutch and reminiscent of the flavours in much of the heartland country cooking. She uses two dressings for the hot noodle salad – a mayonnaise one and a mixture of oil, sugar, and vinegar. The baked orzo with two kinds of peppers is definitely an international offering. Here Helen Witty combines the very small pasta orzo with two kinds of cheese, sour cream, and mild green chilies, producing a casserole with a distinctive Californian-Mexican flavour.

Although Italians usually serve flat pasta with cream so that the sauce clings more easily, Helen Witty's non-traditional Menu 2 calls for round spaghettini mixed with caviar and heavy cream. The trimmings for the caviar are unusual – instead of the typical minced onions, Helen Witty sprinkles snips of green chives over the dish; and instead of passing the sieved egg yolk in a bowl on the side, she tosses it with the pasta and caviar when serving.

Decorate the hot noodle salad, served on a bed of lettuce, with a border of cherry tomatoes and thin radish slices. You can pass the courgette strips vinaigrette on individual salad plates and the breadsticks in a napkin-lined basket. Tumblers of white wine complete the table setting.

Hot Sweet-and-Sour Curly Noodle and Ham Salad
Courgette Strips Vinaigrette

This pasta salad, served hot, makes a complete family meal. The broad curly noodles, made from egg dough, add a distinctive rich flavour to this dish. Their curly shape has an added advantage, because the ruffled edges keep the noodles separate rather than let them clump together after cooking. The contrast in tastes – the pungency of the vinaigrette with the deep, satisfying smoky ham – is refreshing and interesting to serve, too: a plate of this hot, ruffly pasta on a bed of lettuce with tomato wedges is perfectly pitched for a plentiful meal.

Choose a full-flavoured country ham for the salad. If country ham is not available, substitute thin strips of a spicy cooked corned beef.

For a side dish, you use courgette strips with a mild, lemony vinaigrette that accents rather than competes with the main-dish dressing.

What to drink
A crisp French Chablis would best accompany the medley of flavours here. If you prefer a light red wine, your options are international: a light Zinfandel from California, a French Beaujolais, or an Italian Chianti.

Start-to-Finish Steps
1   Follow pasta recipe steps 1 to 7.
2   Follow courgette recipe steps 1 to 3.
3   Follow pasta recipe step 8.
4   Juice lemon for courgette recipe and follow courgette recipe steps 4 and 5.
5   Thinly shred lettuce for pasta recipe. Follow pasta recipe steps 9 to 11, and follow courgette recipe step 6. Serve.

Hot Sweet-and-Sour Curly Noodle and Ham Salad

250 g (¹/₂ lb) cooked smoked ham, thinly sliced
8 to 10 scallions
1 small sweet green or red pepper
2 stalks celery
8 to 10 radishes
Salt
175 g (6 oz) curly egg noodles
125 g (4 oz) mayonnaise
60 ml (2 fl oz) corn or peanut oil
2 level tablespoons dark brown sugar
60 ml (2 fl oz) cider vinegar
Freshly ground black pepper

¹/₂ head iceberg lettuce, thinly shredded
500 g (1 lb) cherry tomatoes

1   Bring water to a boil in stockpot for pasta.
2   Cut ham into thin ribbons.
3   Trim scallions and slice white parts into 5 mm (¹/₄ inch) rounds and green parts into thin slices.
4   Stem and seed pepper and cut into thin strips.
5   Slice celery into thin diagonal strips.
6   Trim radishes and slice into thin rounds.
7   When water boils, add 2 teaspoons salt, then sprinkle in noodles. Cook noodles 7 to 8 minutes.
8   Drain noodles and combine in large bowl with mayonnaise; cover, and keep warm in oven.
9   Heat oil over medium heat, add white part of scallions and pepper strips, and stir until slightly softened, about 2 minutes. Add sugar and vinegar and stir until sugar dissolves and liquid comes to a boil. Remove from heat and season.
10 Using spatula, fold hot vegetables and cooking liquid into noodles, then fold in ham, celery, and radishes. Taste and adjust seasonings, adding salt, pepper, mayonnaise or vinegar as needed.
11 Arrange lettuce on platter. Heap warm salad on lettuce, and garnish with scallion tops and tomatoes.

Courgette Strips Vinaigrette

4 courgettes (about 625 g (1¹/₄ lbs))
Salt
1¹/₂ teaspoons chopped fresh basil, or ¹/₂ tsp dried
1 teaspoon Dijon mustard
Juice of ¹/₂ lemon (about 1¹/₂ tbsps), or more to taste
60 ml (2 fl oz) olive oil
Freshly ground black pepper

1   Bring 2¹/₂ cm (1 inch) of water to a boil.
2   Meanwhile, scrub and trim courgette and cut lengthwise into 1 cm (¹/₂ inch) strips.
3   When water boils, lay courgette strips in skillet, salt lightly, and sprinkle with basil. Cover and cook over medium heat 4 to 6 minutes, or until barely tender; do not overcook.
4   While courgettes cook, whisk together mustard, lemon juice, oil, salt, and pepper until well mixed.
5   Pour off liquid from courgettes, leaving strips in skillet. Set aside, uncovered, until serving time.
6   Pour in vinaigrette and baste once or twice in skillet. Arrange on platter.

Spaghettini in Cream with Red Caviar
Escarole and Mushroom Salad

The flavour of red salmon caviar compares favourably with expensive caviars. If you are concerned about cost, you can use use the still less expensive red or black lumpfish caviar. But no matter which one you use, you should be able to find these caviars in the gourmet food section of your supermarket. If fresh chives, which give this dish its mild oniony taste, are not available, use six to eight tablespoons of scallion leaves, finely minced.

Escarole is a tart salad green – if you prefer a milder taste, you can substitute any lettuce, or combination of salad greens, for the escarole.

What to drink
With caviar you can choose a very plain or a very fancy wine. A good, bone-dry Muscadet, would be plain but enjoyable. Or buy a dry sparkling wine.

Start-to-Finish Steps
1 Follow pasta recipe steps 1 and 2.
2 Juice lemon for pasta recipe, and follow pasta recipe steps 3 and 4.
3 Follow salad recipe steps 1 to 5.
4 Follow pasta recipe steps 5 to 7, and serve.

Spaghettini in Cream with Red Caviar

4 eggs
4 level tablespoons butter
175 ml (6 fl oz) heavy cream
Freshly ground black pepper
2 tablespoons lemon juice
1 tablespoon salt
500 g (1 lb) spaghettini
250 g (8 oz) red salmon caviar
4 to 6 level tablespoons snipped fresh chives

1 Bring water to a boil in stockpot for pasta.
2 Cover eggs with water and set over medium-high heat. When boiling, reduce heat and simmer eggs 10 minutes, until hard-boiled. Drain and cool.
3 Meanwhile, melt butter in small saucepan. Stir in cream and pepper. Heat just to simmering, turn off heat, add lemon juice, and keep warm.
4 When pasta water boils, add salt, then spaghettini, stirring. Cook 8 to 10 minutes, or until barely tender.
5 Shell eggs, cut in half, and remove yolks. Finely chop whites and reserve. Push yolks through sieve.

6 Drain pasta in colander, pouring some of the cooking water into shallow serving bowl to heat it. Empty bowl and tip pasta into it. Add cream mixture and toss thoroughly.
7 Arrange caviar in centre of spaghettini. Sprinkle egg yolk in ring around caviar. Sprinkle chopped egg white around egg yolk. Surround egg with ring of chives. Toss well just before serving.

Escarole and Mushroom Salad

1 head escarole
250 g (½ lb) fresh mushrooms
60 ml (2 fl oz) tarragon white wine vinegar
½ teaspoon salt
Freshly ground black pepper
15 g (½ oz) minced fresh parsley
125 ml (4 fl oz) olive oil

1 Pull escarole apart; wash and dry leaves. Tear into bite-size pieces and roll in towel.
2 Wipe mushrooms and trim stem ends.
3 Combine vinegar, seasoning, and stir until salt dissolves. Add parsley and oil, whisk until blended.
4 Slice mushrooms through cap and stem and put in bowl with dressing. Turn until well coated.
5 Heap escarole over mushrooms and dressing and refrigerate until serving time; then toss thoroughly.

Choose a large plate to serve the spaghettini with sieved egg yolk and red caviar. You can also use a large serving platter and toss the pasta at the table, then add the vinaigrette to the escarole and mushroom salad.

An Abundant Antipasto
Baked Orzo with Peppers and Cheese

Carefully arrange the antipasto on individual plates and serve it before or with the main course of orzo with green chilies.

Most Italian meals begin with an antipasto, or a 'course before the pasta,' which may offer thousands of combinations, both hot and cold, of fish, meats, cheeses, and raw and cooked vegetables – all beautifully arranged. The antipasto in this menu contains many salad-like ingredients, and you could treat this either as an appetizer or as a salad to be eaten along with the main course. However you serve it, offer bread sticks or warmed Italian whole wheat bread to go with it.

Orzo is a Greek pasta shaped like rice and usually served in soups or as an accompaniment for lamb. But, since it is quick cooking and holds its shape well, it is equally suitable for casseroles. For variation, you may substitute small elbow macaroni, or other small pasta shapes such as tubetti or tubettini. The distinctive Mexican flavour comes from combining sour cream, mature cheddar cheese, and mild green chilies. Canned green chilies are available either in the Mexican food section of your supermarket or in a speciality food shop. The flavour of this casserole improves if you cool it slightly before serving. You can let it sit 10 to 15 minutes.

What to drink

This is a country-style menu, and the wines should be Italian. Try a red Montepulciano d'Abruzzo from the south of Italy or a Barbera from the north – both dry and berrylike in flavour. A California Barbera would also do.

Start-to-Finish Steps

1 Follow pasta recipe steps 1 and 2.
2 As water comes to boil, dice mature cheddar and red peppers and grate Parmesan cheese for pasta recipe.
3 Follow pasta recipe steps 3 to 5.
4 Follow antipasto recipe steps 1 to 6, and serve with pasta.

An Abundant Antipasto

1 head crisp curly leaf lettuce
1 bunch watercress (optional)
1 medium-size plum tomato
8 to 12 scallions
8 to 12 radishes
175 g (6 oz) jar marinated artichoke hearts
200 g (7 oz) can tuna packed in olive oil
2 cans rolled anchovy fillets
8 to 12 large green Spanish olives
12 to 16 imported black olives
8 to 12 slices prosciutto
8 slices Italian dry salami
1 level tablespoon capers
125 ml (4 fl oz) olive oil
125 ml (4 fl oz) red wine vinegar
Freshly ground black pepper

1 Wash and dry lettuce and watercress; discard any damaged portions. Spin dry.

2 Rinse, stem, and cut plum tomato into 8 slices.

3 Wash and trim scallions and radishes, retaining several inches of green on scallions. Halve radishes. Dry scallions and radishes.

4 Drain artichoke hearts, tuna, anchovy fillets, and olives; reserve these ingredients separately.

5 Tear lettuce into bite-size pieces and make a generous bed on each of 4 salad plates. Place an equal portion of artichoke hearts and tuna opposite each other on plates. Roll prosciutto slices loosely into cigar shapes and put 2 or 3 rolls on one side of plate, halfway between tuna and artichokes. Roll salami similarly and place 2 rolls opposite prosciutto. Place scallions between prosciutto rolls. In the remaining spaces on plate, decoratively arrange rolled-up anchovy fillets, green and black olives, and radish halves. Sprinkle a few capers over tuna. Tuck bite-size pieces of watercress around antipasto, if desired. Finally, place 2 slices of tomato in the centre of each plate.

6 Serve with cruets of olive oil and red wine vinegar, and pass pepper mill.

Baked Orzo with Peppers and Cheese

2 teaspoons salt
150 g (5 oz) orzo
60 g (2 oz) diced roasted red peppers (use the remaining peppers in antipasto)
45 g (1¹/₂ oz) diced green chilies, or more to taste
125 g (4 oz) diced mature cheddar cheese
250 ml (8 fl oz) sour cream
60 g (2 oz) freshly grater Parmesan cheese
2 level tablespoons butter, cut into small bits

1 Preheat oven to 230°C (450°F or Mark 8).

2 Bring water to a boil in stockpot for pasta.

3 When water boils, add 2 teaspoons salt and sprinkle in orzo. When boiling resumes, cook briskly 10 to 12 minutes, or until just tender; drain.

4 Put orzo in lightly buttered gratin dish or baking pan with peppers, chilies, and mature cheddar. Spread sour cream evenly over top. Sprinkle on Parmesan, then dot with butter.

5 Bake on upper shelf of oven about 15 minutes, or until top is golden and puffy and mixture is bubbling around edges. Remove from oven and let cool slightly.

Added touch

This wine and citrus-scented gelatin dessert has a dark amber colour and looks pretty with its chilled cream topping. If you use a sweet Marsala, reduce the quantity of sugar by one tablespoon. When you serve the dessert, pass the chilled cream in a pitcher and serve crisp wafers or cookies with it.

Marsala Jelly with Chilled Cream

1¹/₂ teaspoons unflavoured gelatin
6 tablespoons cold water
250 ml (8 fl oz) plus 2 tablespoons dry or sweet Marsala
3 tablespoons strained fresh orange juice
2 tablespoons strained fresh lemon juice
250 g (8 oz) sugar
Pinch of salt
250 ml (8 fl oz) heavy cream, chilled

1 Sprinkle gelatin over cold water in small metal saucepan and let soak 5 minutes.

2 In bowl, stir together Marsala, orange juice, lemon juice, sugar, and salt. Stir until all grains of sugar and salt have been dissolved.

3 Set pan with soaked gelatin over very low heat and stir continuously until gelatin has dissolved.

4 Stir gelatin thoroughly into Marsala mixture. Divide among 4 small individual dessert glasses. Cool, then chill until jelly has set. Serve Marsala jelly with heavy cream.

Alfredo Viazzi

Menu 1
(*Right*)
Spaghettini with Sausage and Courgette
String Bean Salad with Nuts and Cream

Liguria, on the Gulf of Genoa on the northern most coast of western Italy, claims credit for the creation of two internationally popular and classic dishes – the rich vegetable-and-pasta soup called minestrone, and ravioli, in particular the special ones filled with minced veal, pork, egg, and Parmesan cheese. A famous culinary centre, Liguria has a rich local cuisine based on a liberal use of herbs. Basil, which flourishes in the hills of the region, is a familiar flavouring in many Ligurian dishes.

Alfredo Viazzi, who lives in New York, acquired both his love of food and his basic training in his native Liguria, which glorifies a simple, hearty way of cooking and eating.

He was taught that there really is no such thing as a dish too plain to be good and that even a well-cooked meal of potatoes and onions can be delicious. Now, as a restaurant owner, he believes that above all, good food should entertain people and be pleasing to look at as well as to taste. And, without being overwhelming, his menus have a certain lavish quality, either in the richness of ingredients or in the unusual combinations of such ingredients as fresh beans, nutmeg, nuts, and cream (see Menu 1), that makes them festive indeed.

Each of his menus is as suitable for guests as for home-style meals. In the manner of Ligurian cooking, recipes in Menu 1 and Menu 3 call for basil, which should be fresh to capture its authentic flavour. Menu 2 features fresh scallops with linguine, served with a rich creamy sauce.

This meal will taste best when courgette and green beans are at their prime, in mid- to late summer. Serve the spaghettini, topped with crumbled sausage and mushroom and courgette slices, and the string beans with nuts and cream on the side.

12

13

Spaghettini with Sausage and Courgettes
String Bean Salad with Nuts and Cream

The main dish here is spaghettini with sausage and courgettes in an olive oil-based tomato sauce. This taste is refreshingly light when paired with a thin spaghetti. Italian parsley, also an ingredient in the sauce, is the ubiquitous herb that Italians use liberally for seasoning. Also known as plain leaf or flat parsley, Italian parsley is more fragrant and flavourful than the familiar curly parsley. If your market does not carry Italian parsley, you can substitute curly parsley, but, for an extra touch of flavour, add a bit of the tender stems, finely minced.

During tomato season, you may want to use fresh rather than canned Italian, or plum, tomatoes. To peel them quickly, drop them in boiling water for several seconds, then scoop them out with a large slotted spoon and rinse them under cold water. When the tomatoes are cool enough to handle, peel them with a sharp knife and proceed with the recipe.

The string bean salad calls for walnuts, and a sprinkling of freshly grated nutmeg, as popular in Italy as elsewhere, gives the salad zest. Look for whole nutmegs on the spice shelves of your supermarket. As good cooks know, freshly grated nutmeg is more pungent than pre-ground – and the grating takes almost no time.

For delicious fresh green beans, select only those that are unblemished, tender, young, and crisp enough to snap when you bend them. Rinse them under cold water after cooking and then be sure to let the cream with nuts and spices cool before you add the beans. The salad tastes best either warm or at room temperature.

What to drink

The harmony of flavours here allows a wide range of choice of red wine. From the north and south of Italy, respectively, a good Chianti or a young Taurasi, or a reasonably priced Merlot from California, would all offer the right degree of fruitiness and dryness.

Start-to-Finish Steps

1 Chop parsley for pasta recipe, and grate nutmeg for pasta and salad recipes. Follow pasta recipe steps 1 to 10.
2 Chop nuts and juice and peel lemon for salad recipe, and follow salad recipe steps 1 to 3.
3 Follow pasta recipe step 11.
4 Grate Parmesan cheese and follow pasta recipe step 12.
5 Follow salad recipe step 4, and serve with pasta.

Spaghettini with Sausage and Courgettes

$^1/_2$ small onion
1 clove garlic
100 ml (3 fl oz) olive oil
2 level tablespoons butter
1 level tablespoon chopped fresh Italian parsley
350 g (12 oz) Italian peeled tomatoes
Pinch of marjoram
Salt
Freshly ground black pepper
3 to 4 fresh basil leaves, or $^1/_4$ teaspoon chopped dried
3 medium-size courgettes (about500g (1 lb))
4 fresh mushrooms
500 g (1 lb) sweet Italian sausages
60 ml (2 fl oz) vegetable oil
Pinch of freshly grated nutmeg
3 tablespoons red wine
500 g (1 lb) spaghettini
5 level tablespoons freshly grated Parmesan cheese

1 Chop both onion and garlic finely.
2 Heat half of the oil in non-aluminium saucepan over medium flame. Add butter, wait 1 minute until it melts, and add onion, garlic, and parsley. Lower flame, stir, and cook about 5 minutes, or until softened.
3 Set stockpot of salted water over low flame to bring to a boil for spaghettini.
4 To saucepan with onion-and-garlic mixture, add tomatoes and break them up. Mix well. Add marjoram, salt, and pepper, and taste for seasoning. Add basil. Cook over low flame 25 minutes, stirring often.
5 Wash courgettes under cold water and pat dry. Slice into $2^1/_2$ mm ($^1/_8$ inch) rounds. Set aside.
6 Lightly rinse mushrooms and pat dry. Thinly slice caps and stems.
7 Take sausage meat out of casings and loosen it with your hands.
8 Heat vegetable oil in skillet over medium flame

and sauté courgettes, stirring until golden brown. Drain on paper towels. Wipe out skillet.

9 Add the remaining olive oil to same skillet and sauté sausage meat until brown, stirring with spoon to crumble into small pieces. Add mushrooms, salt, pepper, and nutmeg. Mix gently. Add wine and let it evaporate. Taste for seasoning.

10 Add courgettes and sausage mixture to tomato sauce and blend well. Taste. Let sauce simmer over low flame.

11 Drop spaghettini into boiling water and loosen it up with long fork. Cook about 7 minutes, or until done. Drain well in colander.

12 Remove sauce from flame and pour half of it into large serving bowl. Transfer spaghettini to bowl and toss well. Add the remaining sauce to pasta and toss again. Pass Parmesan cheese and pepper mill.

String Bean Salad with Nuts and Cream

Juice and rind of $1/2$ lemon
Salt
500 g (1 lb) fresh green beans
2 teaspoons butter
1 level tablespoon coarsely chopped walnuts
125 ml (4 fl oz) heavy cream
Pinch of freshly grated nutmeg
White pepper

1 Bring small amount of water to a boil in medium-size saucepan to which lemon juice, rind, and pinch of salt have been added.

2 Trim beans and cook 8 minutes, or until just tender. Drain well and cool under cold water. Drain again.

3 Melt butter in small saucepan and cook chopped nuts 5 minutes, stirring and shaking pan so they do

not stick to bottom. Add cream and nutmeg and bring to a boil. Remove from heat and keep warm.

4 When ready to serve, add salt and pepper to cream dressing and pour over beans. Mix well.

Added touch

If you have some extra time and wish to make an elegant appetizer, try peppers stuffed with cubed lamb, pine nuts, and other savoury ingredients. Although it is easy to follow, it is a lengthy recipe that requires about an hour of preparation time.

Stuffed Peppers Saturnia

6 small sweet red or yellow peppers
6 level tablespoons butter
2 tablespoons dry vermouth
Salt
Freshly ground black pepper
Rind of $1/2$ lemon, chopped very fine
750 g ($1^1/2$ lbs) boneless lean lamb
1 egg yolk
3 tablespoons heavy cream
2 level tablespoons freshly grated Parmesan cheese
$1/2$ packet saffron
2 tablespoons water
Pinch of turmeric
2 level tablespoons chopped pine nuts
$1/2$ tablespoon freshly chopped Italian parsley
125 ml (4 fl oz) chicken stock

1 Preheat oven to 190°C (375°F or Mark 5).

2 Core and seed peppers. Rinse and let drain, open side down.

3 Melt butter over low flame and mix in vermouth. Simmer 2 minutes. Turn peppers cut side up, shaving off thin slice from bottoms so they stand flat. Pour mixture evenly into peppers, swirl around to coat insides of peppers, and allow to marinate for $1/2$ hour.

4 Drain excess butter-and-vermouth mixture into skillet. Heat, and add salt and pepper. Add lamb and lemon rind. Cook over medium flame, about 20 minutes. Remove lamb and chop into small pieces. Let cool.

5 In medium-size bowl, combine chopped lamb, egg yolk beaten into heavy cream, Parmesan cheese, saffron diluted in 2 tablespoons of warm water, turmeric, parsley, and chopped pine nuts. Mix well, taste, and set aside.

6 Place peppers, open side up, in baking pan, and add chicken stock. Bake 10 minutes. Remove peppers and stuff with mixture. Arrange peppers, stuffed side up, in same baking pan. Replace in oven. Bake additional 15 minutes. Remove and place under grill $1^1/2$ minutes.

Linguine with Scallops
Broccoli Salad

Recipes with shellfish are characteristic of Ligurian cooking, but such seasonings as nutmeg, ginger, and white pepper are untypical. Here, as Alfredo Viazzo inventively combines them in the scallop marinade and the linguine sauce, these spices add a piquant and distinctive flavour to the pasta dish.

The scallops we eat are thick muscles that open and close the familiar ripped shells. Scallops come in two varieties: the often preferred tiny, tender bay scallop and the larger, firmer sea scallop. When selecting scallops, check them for a clean sea-air odour and firm flesh.

The success of the salad depends upon your using broccoli that is both very fresh and crisp. When you shop for this recipe, select a bunch of broccoli with a rich green colour, compact buds in the head, and firm stalks. Anchovies, tiny fish with a pungent flavour, are available packed either in salt or oil. Salt-packed anchovies, usually found in Italian groceries, are preferable, but must be cleaned under cold water, skinned, and boned before use. However, you can certainly use oil-packed anchovies, which are sold in tins or jars. When a recipe calls for using only a few anchovy fillets – as this one does – remove the required amount, drain the fillets on paper towels, and store the rest in the closed jar in the refrigerator.

What to drink
Scallops need a rich, dry white wine to complement them. A dry California Gewurztraminer or a good Chardonnay (from Italy or California) or a white Burgundy (a Rully or a Saint-Véran) would all do nicely. Serve the wine very cold. A sparkling mineral water also makes a pleasant accompaniment, whether or not you serve wine.

Start-to-Finish Steps
1   Peel lemon for salad recipe and juice lemon for pasta and salad recipes.
2   Follow pasta recipe steps 1 to 3.
3   Follow broccoli recipe steps 1 and 2.
4   Chop garlic, parsley, and anchovies for broccoli recipe and follow broccoli recipe step 3.
5   Grate Parmesan cheese, if using, and follow pasta recipe steps 4 to 8. Serve with broccoli salad.

A dish of linguine, tossed together with scallops and garnished with chopped parsley, and a side dish of broccoli florets make an attractive meal. For an elegant touch, serve the wine from a glass decanter.

Linguine with Scallops

500 g (1 lb) fresh bay scallops
Juice of $1/2$ lemon (about 2 tablespoons)
1 bunch fresh Italian parsley
1 large clove garlic
Pinch of freshly grated nutmeg
Pinch of ground ginger
Salt
Freshly ground white pepper
500 g (1 lb) linguine
5 level tablespoons butter
60 ml (2 fl oz) heavy cream
30 g (1 oz) freshly grated Parmesan cheese for garnish
   (optional)

1 Set stockpot of salted water over low flame to bring to a boil for pasta.
2 Wash scallops thoroughly under cold water and drain well. Place scallops in bowl and add lemon juice.
3 Chop enough parsley to yield $1/2$ tablespoon. Chop garlic. Grate nutmeg. Add parsley, garlic, nutmeg, ginger, salt, and white pepper to mixing bowl. Toss well. Taste marinade and adjust seasonings. Let scallops sit in marinade until ready to cook.
4 When water boils, drop linguine into water and loosen up with fork. Cook 7 or 8 minutes, or until done.
5 While pasta is cooking, melt butter in skillet. Drain scallops from marinade and sauté them 3 to 4 minutes, making sure to coat well with butter. Add cream and reduce, 1 minute. Taste. Add salt and pepper if needed.
6 Drain linguine when cooked *al dente*.
7 Set skillet over medium flame and wait 1 minute; then add linguine to scallop sauce. Blend thoroughly. Stir about 2 minutes.
8 Serve hot, distributing scallops as evenly as possible. Serve Parmesan cheese on the side, if desired, and pass pepper mill.

Broccoli Salad

1 bunch broccoli
Juice and rind of $1/2$ lemon
125 ml (4 fl oz) olive oil
1 tablespoon red wine vinegar
$1/2$ tablespoon chopped fresh Italian parsley
5 anchovy fillets, finely chopped
$1/2$ teaspoon Dijon mustard
$1/4$ teaspoon chopped garlic
Freshly ground black pepper

1 Cut broccoli into florets with $2^{1/2}$ cm (1 inch) stems. Wash and drain them.
2 Cook broccoli about 4 minutes in boiling salted water to which lemon juice and rind have been added. Keep broccoli gently pressed down in water. Drain in colander and run under cold water. Shake broccoli gently to remove all water.
3 Mix the remaining ingredients in serving bowl and add broccoli. Toss gently to coat florets. Let stand at room temperature until ready to serve.

Pasticcio di Lasagnette
Arugula Salad

The baked pasticcio – lasagnette that is layered with meat, cheese and vegetables – with an arugula salad is an informal meal.

Outside an Italian kitchen, *pasticcio* means 'mess.' To an Italian cook, a pasticcio is a dish that combines cooked pasta with cheese, vegetables, or meat, all bound together by eggs or a cream sauce. Often a pasticcio bakes without a crust, but this recipe calls for a layering of cheese slices, which form a bubbly crust when they melt. Though the dish is basically uncomplicated, it has a multiplicity of ingredients. Before you begin to follow the recipe, collect all the ingredients from the pantry and refrigerator and line them up in order on your work surface. Then proceed with making the recipe.

Arugula (see drawing) is an Italian salad green. It has narrow frilled leaves and a distinctive peppery bite, not unlike watercress. If you have difficulty finding arugula, you can use either watercress or any field salad greens. Before using, arugula must be rinsed thoroughly to remove any sand, then drained, and gently patted dry.

What to drink
This interesting version of a classic Italian dish calls for a classic Italian wine – a full-bodied Chianti Classico *riserva.* As an alternative, try a young, medium-priced Barbaresco, a red wine from the Piedmont, or a California merlot.

Start-to-Finish Steps

1   Chop parsley and basil, grate nutmeg and Parmesan cheese, and wash and scrape carrot and celery for pasta recipe. Slice Fontina for pasta recipe.
2   Follow pasta recipe steps 1 to 13.
3   As pasta bakes, chop garlic if using it, and follow salad recipe steps 1 and 2.
4   Serve pasta and salad.

Pasticcio di Lasagnette

6 pieces dry *porcini* mushrooms
125 ml (4 fl oz) beef broth
1 small onion
1 carrot, washed and scraped
1 stalk celery, washed and scraped
2 level tablespoons salt
60 ml (2 fl oz) plus 2 tablespoons olive oil
125 g (4 oz) butter
$1/_2$ tablespoon chopped fresh Italian parsley
$1^1/_2$ teaspoons chopped fresh basil, or $1/_2$ teaspoon dried
3 tablespoons red wine
30 g (1 oz) flour
250 ml (8 fl oz) plus 2 tablespoons heavy cream
Salt
Pinch of freshly grated nutmeg
Pinch of ground ginger
100 g (3 oz) freshly grated Parmesan cheese

500 g (1 lb) lean chopped beef
2 level tablespoons tomato paste
2 tablespoons water
Freshly ground black pepper
500 g (1 lb) lasagnette, fresh or dried
350 g (³/₄ lb) fresh spinach
125 g (¹/₄ lb) mortadella or boiled ham, thinly sliced
125 g (¹/₄ lb) Fontina, mozzarella, or other soft
   cheese, thinly sliced

1 Preheat oven to 190°C (375°F or Mark 5).
2 Wash mushrooms well under lukewarm water, and then soak them in beef broth until ready to use.
3 Purée onion, carrot, and celery together in food processor.
4 Bring water and 2 tablespoons salt to a boil in stockpot or kettle over medium flame for pasta.
5 Heat 60 ml (2 fl oz) of the olive oil in saucepan and melt 15 g (¹/₂ oz) of the butter in it. Add vegetable mixture, parsley, and basil. Cook 5 to 6 minutes, stirring, or until vegetables are softened. Add red wine and cook until it evaporates, about 2 minutes.
6 Add chopped beef and amalgamate well with all other ingredients. Cook over low flame, stirring occasionally.
7 Melt 75 g (2¹/₂ oz) of the butter in another saucepan over medium flame. Add flour and blend well with whisk. Cook until it becomes deep yellow mixture. Add cream, a bit at a time, and keep blending. Add pinch of salt, nutmeg, and ginger. Add 30 g (1 oz) of the Parmesan cheese. Blend well and keep warm. This is called béchamel sauce.
8 Remove mushrooms from their soaking liquid and coarsely chop them. Then add mushrooms and beef broth to chopped beef. Mix. Add tomato paste diluted in 2 tablespoons warm water. Blend well. Lower flame and let sauce simmer. Add salt and pepper. Taste and adjust seasonings if necessary. This is called Bolognese sauce.
9 At this point, water for pasta should be boiling. Drop in lasagnette. Cook fresh lasagnette 2 to 3 minutes or dry lasagnette about 7 minutes.
10 Wash spinach thoroughly under cold water and cut off tough stems. Steam spinach in small amount of water for 2 minutes. Drain well and chop coarsely.
11 Drain pasta well in colander. Put back in pot and add the remaining 2 tablespoons olive oil. Toss to coat well.
12 Coat baking pan with the remaining butter. Lay half of the lasagnette in pan and pour Bolognese sauce over it. Shower with 30 g (1 oz) of the Parmesan cheese. Place slices of mortadella or ham over cheese. Lay the remaining lasagnette over mortadella. Cover with chopped spinach; smooth top. Pour béchamel sauce over spinach. Smooth. Sprinkle with the remaining Parmesan cheese. Arrange slices of Fontina or other cheese over béchamel.
13 Place pan in oven and bake 15 to 20 minutes. Cut into 4 portions to serve.

Arugula Salad

2 bunches arugula or watercress
2 tablespoons olive oil
¹/₂ lemon
Salt
Freshly ground black pepper
Touch of chopped garlic (optional)

1 Cut off tough stems and wash arugula or watercress thoroughly under cold water. Drain well and arrange in serving bowl.
2 Pour olive oil over salad and squeeze lemon juice on it. Add salt, pepper, and garlic if desired. Toss well.

Ed Giobbi

Menu 1
(*Right*)

Spaghettini with Salad Greens
Veal Chops in Paper Bags
Baked Asparagus

Years ago, as an art student on a meagre budget, Ed Giobbi – rather than eating inferior restaurant food – cut costs by cooking family-style, regional Italian meals at home. These menus were based on fresh seasonal vegetables, seafood, and pasta and seasoned simply with herbs – thus he learned that the appeal of authentic Italian cooking lies in its economy and its use of fresh foods. Now an internationally known painter, he still makes time in his day for cooking.

Contrary to the image many Americans have of most Italian food, when properly prepared it requires a minimum of oil and is particularly low-fat (and even a low-calorie) cuisine. Ed Giobbi's three menus highlight both the seasonality and wholesomeness of Italian cooking. Menu 1 and menu 3 are suitable for spring and summer dining: they feature vegetables that reach their flavour peak during warm weather. The salad in Menu 2, an ample winter meal, calls for fresh oranges, which are at their best in Italy in winter. The pasta, meat, and fresh produce in each menu are carefully balanced for nutrition, colour, and flavour.

A native of Connecticut, Ed Giobbi is a first-generation American who nonetheless has lived many years in Italy, travelling throughout the country to familiarize himself with various regional favourites. He specializes in those from central Italy, particularly Abruzzi and the Marches, where seafood stews, grilled meats, and exceptionally good pasta are characteristic.

Dark linens and coordinated dinnerware make an appropriate, home-style backdrop for spaghettini with salad greens, veal chops, and asparagus spears. For a dramatic presentation, leave the veal chops in their paper wrapping and snip each bag open when you serve them. Garnish the baked asparagus with lemon crescents.

Spaghettini with Salad Greens
Veal Chops in Paper Bags
Baked Asparagus

Spaghettini with salad greens is really an appetizer, not a salad, but because it is a light dish, you can feature it as a main luncheon course with an accompanying platter of bread and cheese. If you wish to increase the pasta quantity to provide second helpings, Ed Giobbi suggests you prepare this recipe – as you should all pasta recipes – several times as it is. That way you know what taste to strive for when you increase quantities. Unlike other recipes, pasta with sauce cannot simply be doubled – larger quantities of hot cooked pasta will absorb more liquid, and you must adjust the sauce to provide that moisture.

Cooking food wrapped in paper is an excellent way to retain moisture in delicate lean meats such as veal and chicken. Before paper wrapping the chops, trim off any excess fat, then shake them in a sealed paper bag with flour to coat them. When you are ready to fill the paper bags for baking, place them in a baking dish in case the bags leak in the oven. Place a chop in each bag, ladle in the sauce, then crimp the tops of the bags closed. Rubbing the bags with oil helps to prevent their scorching. As the meat cooks, excess steam evaporates, causing the bags to rise and puff up. Serve the meal with the bags intact; snipping them open at the table releases an appetizing aroma. Paper bags are readily available and easy to use, but make sure you use clean, brown ones. You can use kitchen parchment instead, but avoid using foil, which traps the steam.

The asparagus bakes in an olive-based sauce. Since the distinctive flavour of the oil is important to the success of this recipe, select an imported extra virgin olive oil.

What to drink

The richly flavoured sauce on the veal chops here calls for a light and elegant red wine – a young Taurasi or a young Barbaresco, or light Cabernet or Merlot from California. A good white Graves is another alternative.

Start-to-Finish Steps

1 Slice mushrooms and chop shallots, scallions, and rosemary for veal recipe. Chop parsley and mince garlic for veal and asparagus recipes. Follow veal recipe steps 1 to 6.

2 Follow pasta recipe steps 1 and 2.
3 Wedge lemon for asparagus recipe. Follow asparagus recipe steps 1 and 2.
4 As asparagus bakes, follow veal recipe step 7.
5 As veal bakes, follow pasta recipe steps 3 to 5.
6 Follow veal recipe step 8, and follow asparagus recipe step 3. Serve both with pasta salad.

Spaghettini with Salad Greens

1 head curly lettuce
1 head escarole
1 head Belgian endive
1 bunch arugula or watercress
350 g (³/₄ lb) spaghettini
3 tablespoons olive oil
60 ml (2 fl oz) wine vinegar
¹/₂ teaspoon minced garlic (optional)
Freshly ground black pepper
Salt

1 Bring water to a boil in large stockpot for pasta.
2 Wash greens, drain, and spin dry. Tear into bite-size pieces. There should be approximately 350 g (12 oz) torn salad greens. Greens should be at room temperature.
3 Cook pasta in boiling salted water 5 to 7 minutes, or until *al dente*.
4 Mix oil, vinegar, and garlic, if desired, in cup or bowl.
5 When pasta is cooked, drain well in colander and put in serving bowl with salad greens. Pour dressing over pasta and toss well. Add salt and pepper to taste.

Veal Chops in Paper Bags

4 veal chops, each about 2¹/₂ cm (1 inch) thick
Salt
Freshly ground black pepper
30 g (1 oz) flour, for dredging
60 ml (2 fl oz) olive oil
3 level tablespoons butter
250 g (¹/₂ lb) sliced fresh mushrooms

1½ tablespoons chopped shallots
2 cloves garlic, minced
60 g (2 oz) coarsely chopped scallions
1 tablespoon chopped fresh rosemary, or 1 teaspoon dried
175 ml (6 fl oz) Marsala, or sweet sherry
3 tablespoons chicken broth
4 level tablespoons chopped fresh Italian parsley

1 Preheat oven to 200°C (400°F or Mark 6).
2 Sprinkle chops with salt and pepper and dredge in flour, shaking off excess.
3 Heat oil and butter in skillet large enough to hold chops in 1 layer, or use 2 skillets. When oil is very hot, add chops and cook over high heat about 3 minutes, turning constantly until browned. Remove chops from skillet.
4 Lower heat under skillet and add mushrooms, shallots, garlic, scallions, rosemary, salt, and pepper. Stir constantly until mixture begins to brown.
5 Add Marsala, chicken broth, and chops. Cook over high heat until sauce thickens slightly, about 5 minutes. Turn chops over occasionally. When sauce has thickened, turn off heat.
6 Using paper towel, completely grease outside of 4 lunch-size clean, brown paper bags to prevent bags from charrring.
7 Gently place 1 chop in each bag, and then put mushrooms and sauce on top of each chop. Sprinkle 1 tablespoon of the parsley on each chop. Crimp bags and place in baking dish. Bake 10 to 15 minutes, depending on how pink you like veal.
8 Serve chops in paper bags, opening bags at table.

Baked Asparagus

500g (1 lb) fresh asparagus
2 small cloves garlic, minced
Salt
Freshly ground black pepper
4 level tablespoons chopped fresh Italian parsley
3 tablespoons olive oil
4 lemon wedges

1 Preheat oven to 200°C (400°F or Mark 6).
2 Wash and drain asparagus. Cut off and discard tough ends. Place asparagus tightly together in baking pan. Sprinkle with garlic, salt, pepper, parsley, and oil. Bake uncovered until asparagus is firm to the bite, 15 to 20 minutes, depending on thickness.
3 Serve with lemon wedges.

Added touch
This cake, which takes about an hour to make – including baking time – calls for fresh seasonal fruit, and you can vary the fruit combination to suit your taste.

Torta di frutta

The filling:
125 ml (4 fl oz) milk
1 egg
100 ml (3 fl oz) vegetable oil
100g (3 oz) sugar
125 g (4 oz) flour
1½ teaspoons baking powder
½ teaspoon salt

The topping:
125 g (4 oz) sugar
30 g (1 oz) flour
⅛ teaspoon salt
30 g (1 oz) dried lemon peel
2 tablespoons vegetable oil
1 teaspoon lemon juice
175 g (6 oz) fresh seasonal fruit, washed, peeled, and cut into bite-size pieces

1 Preheat oven to 190°C (375°F or Mark 5).
2 For filling, mix together egg, milk, and vegetable oil. Add sugar, and mix until well blended. In separate bowl, mix flour, baking powder, and salt. Add mixture to egg-milk mixture and blend.
3 Grease medium-size baking dish, and add mixture to dish.
4 Make topping by combining sugar, flour, salt, dried lemon peel, vegetable oil, and lemon juice. Mix until well blended.
5 Sprinkle topping on cake batter, then add fresh fruit. Place cake in oven and bake 30 minutes, or until done.

Macaroni Country Style
Orange and Olive Salad

Pass the macaroni country style on a large, plain platter. Put the orange and olive salad in a glass bowl to add bright colour.

The pasta, potato, broccoli, mushrooms, cheese, herbs, and wine in Ed Giobbi's macaroni country-style recipe make an ideal one-pot meal – a gratifying lunch or dinner for a brisk day. Besides being rich in texture and colour, it is nutritionally complete – the broccoli contains vitamins A, and the cheese and ham are rich in protein and together contribute vitamins A, B, and D. The potato adds only a few calories and also contributes calcium and vitamin C.

The combination of potato with pasta is by no means unusual. The idea comes straight from a turn-of-the-century northern Italian cookbook. As practical Italian cooks have always known, pasta cooked in the same water with potato acquires an invisible starchy coating that makes any sauce adhere better. The sauce in this recipe is based on white wine, rather than the more conventional tomato or cream.

The orange and olive salad is a southern Italian speciality from Ed Giobbi's uncle's kitchen. It may have originated centuries ago in Greece and may also owe something to Arab cooking. Southern Italian cooking has ancient connections from all around the

Mediterranean – North Africa and the Middle East, as well as Greece. Leaving the oranges unpeeled not only saves preparation time but adds the pungency of the peel to the salad flavours. You will need a sharp knife and fork for the salad. The cured black olives – Mediterranean favourites – have a wrinkled, almost dried appearance. Additionally, they have a slightly bitter aftertaste that, in this salad, counterbalances the sweetness of the sliced oranges.

What to drink
Serve this meal with simple wines of good quality to show off the virtues of the down-to-earth ingredients. Try a good bottle of Valpolicella or a Beaujolais if you want red wine, Soave or Muscadet if you prefer white.

Start-to-Finish Steps
1 Follow salad recipe steps 1 to 3.
2 Slice mushrooms and onion, chop herbs, grate Parmesan cheese, and cube ham for pasta recipe.
3 Follow pasta recipe steps 1 to 6.
4 Follow salad recipe step 4.
5 Serve pasta and salad.

Macaroni Country Style

Salt
1 bunch broccoli, cut into florets
2 medium-size potatoes
2 tablespoons olive oil
2 level tablespoons butter
1 medium-size onion, thinly sliced
125 g (¹/₄ lb) boiled ham, sliced 1 cm (¹/₂ inch) thick and cut into cubes
60 g (2 oz) sliced mushrooms
Freshly ground black pepper
250 g (¹/₂ lb) rigatoni or other tubular pasta
125 ml (4 fl oz) dry white wine
1¹/₂ teaspoons chopped fresh marjoram, or ¹/₂ teaspoon dried
2 level tablespoons chopped fresh Italian parsley
60 g (2 oz) freshly grated Parmesan cheese

1 In large stockpot, bring salted water to a boil for pasta.
2 Trim broccoli. Peel potatoes and dice them in 5 mm (¹/₄ inch) dices. There should be about 125 g (4 oz).
3 Heat oil and butter in skillet and sauté onion until wilted. Add ham, mushrooms, and pepper, and cook, stirring, 3 or 4 minutes.

4 Add pasta to boiling water.
5 Add wine, marjoram, and 1 tablespoon of the parsley to ham mixture. Cover and simmer over low heat.
6 When pasta has reached a rolling boil, add potatoes and broccoli. Cook until pasta is *al dente*. Drain pasta and vegetables in colander and put in large serving bowl. Add ham sauce and toss well. Add cheese and the remaining parsley.

Orange and Olive Salad

4 navel oranges
125 g (4 oz) dried-cured black olives
1 clove garlic
60 ml (2 fl oz) olive oil
1 bunch watercress for garnish (optional)

1 Wash skins of oranges thoroughly and cut whole oranges into thin slices. Do not peel.
2 Pit olives and cut into 4 pieces. Set aside.
3 Rub salad bowl with peeled garlic and then discard garlic. Arrange orange slices in bowl.
4 Just before serving, add olives and sprinkle with olive oil. Toss gently. Garnish with watercress, if desired.

Added touch
Since the main dish is filling, the best dessert is a bowl of fresh fruit – even though the salad features fruit. Serve pears and apples and, for a nice contrast, try adding some Italian cheeses. Gorgonzola (akin to Roquefort) is traditional with pears, and Bel Paese goes well with tart apples.

Spaghettini Primavera
Fillet of Sole with Vegetables
Baked Spinach

Serve the pasta primavera with the meal or, if you prefer, as a first course while the fillet of sole and the spinach finish cooking.

Spaghettini primavera is a popular late-spring, early summer dish in the central regions of Italy. It combines two Italian favourites: pasta and fresh raw tomatoes. Other versions of this pasta dish can include – in addition to or instead of the tomatoes – a combination of garden-fresh vegetables, available from spring to autumn. (The vegetables for pasta primavera should always be blanched until they are crisp-tender before you add them to the cooked pasta.) Ed Giobbi, who helped to popularize pasta primavera in the United states, says that you should make this dish only when you can purchase the very best, freshest seasonal vegetables.

Sweet and tender fillets of sole take careful handling during and after cooking because they tend to fall apart easily. If fresh sole is not available in your market, you can use other thin white-fleshed fish, such as small bass fillets. Try to avoid using frozen fish – the texture and the taste do not compare to fresh.

A casserole of baked spinach rounds out this well-balanced nutritious meal. Use fresh rather than frozen spinach if possible. You can buy fresh spinach in bulk by the pound or pre-washed in plastic bags. In either case, pick out spinach with crisp, dark-green leaves. Do not buy any that looks wilted. Raw spinach, stored in a plastic bag, keeps for up to five days in the refrigerator. Before cooking the spinach,

immerse it in cold water, rinse it thoroughly, and repeat the process two or three times, tasting a leaf or two at random to make sure the grit is gone. Lemon juice, garlic, and freshly ground black pepper – as in this recipe – are perfect partners for spinach.

What to drink
The pronounced tomato flavour in this menu requires bright, fruity, acidic white wines to match it. Your best choice is from the young Italian white wines, especially the northern Pinot Grigio or the southern Greco di Tufo.

Start-to-Finish Steps
1 Chop garlic, tomatoes, and parsley for pasta recipe.
2 Follow pasta recipe steps 1 and 2.
3 Slice mushrooms, chop scallions and parsley, and cube tomatoes for sole recipe, and follow sole recipe steps 1 to 3.
4 Wash spinach and mince garlic for spinach recipe, and follow spinach recipe steps 1 and 2.
5 As spinach bakes, follow sole recipe step 4.
6 As sole bakes, follow pasta recipe steps 3 and 4.
7 Slice lemons for spinach recipe, and follow spinach recipe step 3; serve with sole and pasta.

Spaghettini Primavera

2 tablespoons salt
1½ teaspoons coarsely chopped garlic
3 tablespoons olive oil
15 g (½ oz) loosely packed fresh basil
3 cups coarsely chopped ripe tomatoes (about 4 medium-size)
1½ tablespoons chopped fresh Italian parsley
Freshly ground black pepper
350 g (¾ lb) spaghettini or linguine

1 Bring water to a boil in stockpot for pasta. Add 2 tablespoons salt.
2 Purée garlic, olive oil, and basil in blender or food processor. Fold in tomatoes and parsley. Or, if you prefer, purée all ingredients together for smoother sauce. Season to taste.
3 Cook pasta in rapidly boiling water, stirring often.
4 When pasta is cooked *al dente*, drain in colander and put in warm serving bowl. Add sauce and blend well. Or put pasta in individual bowls and spoon sauce over, letting each person mix his or her own at table.

Fillet of Sole with Vegetables

1½ level tablespoons butter
4½ tablespoons olive oil
250 g (½ lb) thinly sliced fresh mushrooms
4 fillets of sole or other white-fleshed fish (about 18 cm (7 inches) long
1 lemon
Salt
Freshly ground black pepper
175 g (6 oz) chopped scallions
2 level tablespoons chopped fresh Italian parsley
350 g (12 oz) cubed ripe tomatoes (about 4 medium-size)

1 Preheat oven to 240°C (475°F or Mark 9).
2 Heat butter and 1½ tablespoons oil in skillet and sauté mushrooms until all moisture cooks out.
3 Arrange fish fillets on baking tray in 1 layer. Squeeze lemon juice on each fillet and season with salt and pepper. Sprinkle with dash of olive oil. Spread each fillet with layer of mushrooms, scallions, and parsley and mound of tomatoes. Season again with salt and pepper and then sprinkle with remaining olive oil.
4 Place fish in oven and cook about 6 minutes. Do not overcook. As soon as fish separates, it is done. Remove with long metal turner to be certain fillets remain intact.

Baked Spinach

3 tablespoons olive oil
2 small cloves garlic, minced
1 kg (2 lbs) fresh spinach, well washed and trimmed
Salt
Freshly ground black pepper
4 lemon slices

1 Preheat oven to 240°C (475°F or Mark 9).
2 Pour oil into oven-proof casserole. Add garlic, spinach, salt, and pepper. Cover and bake about 10 minutes, stirring once or twice.
3 Serve with lemon slices.

Added touch
Potato balls make an extra vegetable dish to round out the meal. This recipe calls for pine nuts, which are expensive and often difficult to find. If you wish, you can substitute your favourite nuts for them.

Potato Balls

2 medium-size potatoes (500 g (1 lb))
2½ level tablespoons pine nuts, chopped
½ tablespoon olive oil
1½ level tablespoons chopped Italian parsley
Salt
Freshly ground pepper
Lightly beaten egg white from 1 small egg
Dry unflavoured bread crumbs (about 60 g (2 oz))
Corn oil (about 500 ml (1 pt))
1 lemon, wedged

1 Boil potatoes; peel and mash them.
2 Add pine nuts, olive oil, parsley, salt, and pepper and mix well. Form balls about size of walnuts (1 heaped tablespoon). Roll each ball in egg white, then in bread crumbs.
3 Heat 1½ cm (¾ inch) of corn oil in skillet. When very hot, place some of the potato balls in oil with tongs. If oil is not hot enough, potato balls will fall apart. Cook balls, turning gently with tongs, until golden brown. Drain on paper towels. Repeat process until all potato balls are cooked. Serve with lemon wedges.

Bernice Hunt

Menu 1
(*Left*)
Fresh Figs or Melon with Prosciutto
Cartwheels with Mixed Vegetables

Bernice Hunt, a New York author, not only writes books about food, but also loves to cook for both family and friends. Many of her recipes are inspired by northern Italian cooking, which she grew to love after numerous trips to Bologna, the gastronomic centre of northern Italy. There, the emphasis is on using cheeses, cured hams, delicate pasta, and quality raw ingredients.

As all good cooks do, Bernice Hunt emphasizes using fresh natural ingredients and rarely plans a meal until she visits her local greengrocer. She has not let a busy career interfere with her cooking, but in order to have the time she needs for kitchen creativity, she has learned an economy of motion, making every recipe direct and simple. The menus she presents reflect her no-fuss, Italian-style approach to cooking.

In Menu 1, a light spring or summer meal from northern Italy, fresh figs or melon with sliced prosciutto balance the main pasta course of cartwheels with a sauce replete with chunks of vegetables. The key to the success of this menu is to use fresh, seasonal produce.

By contrast, Menu 2 and Menu 3 require fresh, but not strictly seasonal, produce – such as the carrots for the soup and the mushrooms for the salad in Menu 2, and the broccoli for the vegetable platter in Menu 3. This way you can serve these two meals any time of the year.

Casual pottery serving pieces underline the informality of cantaloupe wedges with prosciutto and cartwheels tossed with bite-size vegetables and Parmesan cheese – a meal best served buffet style, with the cheese grater handy. Fill out the meal with a green salad, if you wish.

Fresh Figs or Melon with Prosciutto
Cartwheels with Mixed Vegetables

This classic Italian appetizer pairs sliced salty prosciutto with fresh, sweet melon slices or whole figs. Italian cooks use a type of cantaloupe that thrives in northern Italy, but honeydew melons are also delicious with prosciutto. If you can find fresh figs, select those that are soft but not mushy and that have unbroken skins. Store them in the refrigerator and use them as soon as possible. For peak flavour, serve figs at room temperature.

Combined with cream and grated Parmesan cheese, a medley of fresh vegetables – leeks, mushrooms, summer-ripe courgettes, and regular or cherry tomatoes – serves as a sauce for the cartwheels. This wheel-shaped pasta is sturdy enough to hold the vegetable-laden sauce. But you can also vary the pasta by using elbows or shells instead – if you do, they should be bite-size for easy eating.

What to drink
Choose a bright, fruity white wine with a bit of spice or a bit of acid flavour: an Italian Pinot Grigio, very young, or a dry California Riesling.

Start-to-Finish Steps
1 Follow pasta recipe steps 1 to 5.
2 As pasta cooks, follow fruit and prosciutto recipe step 1 if using figs or steps 2 and 3 if using melon.
3 Grate Parmesan cheese for pasta recipe and follow pasta recipe steps 6 to 9.
4 Serve fruit and prosciutto.
5 Follow pasta recipe steps 10 and 11.

Fresh Figs or Melon with Prosciutto

8 fresh figs, or 1 ripe melon
8 slices prosciutto
1 bunch watercress, arugula, or parsley for garnish

1 Wash figs and pat them dry. Put 2 on each of 4 serving plates and arrange 2 slices of prosciutto alongside. The perfect garnish is fresh fig leaves, but they are not often included with the figs. Brighten up plate with sprigs of watercress, arugula, or parsley if desired.
2 If using melon, cut in half, remove seeds, and peel.

3 With cut side up, slice each half into uniform crescents about 1 cm ($^1/_2$ inch) thick. Attractively arrange several slices on individual plates – slightly overlapping – and drape 2 slices of prosciutto across top. Garnish with sprigs of watercress, arugula, or parsley, if desired.

Cartwheels with Mixed Vegetables

Salt
2 medium-size leeks
4 level tablespoons butter
1 medium-size courgette
125 g ($^1/_4$ lb) fresh mushrooms
1 large ripe tomato, or 5 to 7 cherry tomatoes
500 g (1 lb) cartwheels or pasta shells
250-350 ml (8-12 fl oz) light cream or half-and-half
125 g (4 oz) freshly grated Parmesan cheese
Freshly ground black pepper

1 Heat water and 1 tablespoon salt in stockpot or kettle for pasta.
2 Clean leeks, separating segments to wash out all sand and grit. Finely chop both white and green parts, discarding only tough ends.
3 Melt butter in skillet. Add chopped leeks and sauté over medium heat about 10 minutes, stirring several times.
4 Scrub and slice courgette. Wipe mushrooms and slice them. Wash and chop tomato.
5 Add pasta to boiling water and cook until just tender, about 15 minutes.
6 Add courgette, mushrooms, and tomato to leeks and stir-fry over fairly high heat until courgette is barely tender; it should remain bright green.
7 Add 250 ml (8 fl oz) of the cream, 60 g (2 oz) of the grated cheese, and salt and pepper to taste. Just before mixture comes to a boil, turn off heat.
8 When pasta is just tender, drain and return to pot.
9 Pour half of the sauce over pasta and stir well; cover and reserve until after appetizer course.
10 When ready to serve, add the remaining sauce to pasta and toss well. Heat briefly over high heat, stirring constantly. If pasta has absorbed too much sauce, add the additional cream.
11 Serve and pass the remaining cheese at table.

Carrot Soup
Fusilli with Chicken and Rosemary

When you serve the soup, garnish each bowl with chopped fresh chives or curly parsley.

Spiral-shaped fusilli has grooves that pick up the cubed chicken and rosemary-flavoured sauce. You can substitute any other grooved pasta.

Rosemary has an intense, pungent flavour, so use cautiously. For maximum flavour, crumble the leaves.

What to drink
These rich flavours need a full-bodied white wine: a California Chardonnay, an Italian Cortese, or a French Mâcon. Whichever you choose, serve it lightly chilled.

Start-to-Finish Steps
1   Follow soup recipe steps 1 to 5.
2   Cut garlic into quarters, chop rosemary, and grate cheese for pasta recipe. Follow pasta recipe steps 1 to 6.
3   Chop chives, and follow soup recipe step 6.
4   Follow pasta recipe steps 7 to 9. Serve.

Carrot Soup

1 bunch carrots (about 500 g (1 lb))
1 large shallot
250 ml (8 fl oz) chicken broth
750 ml-1 ltr (1 1/2-1 3/4 pts) milk
Freshly ground black pepper
Salt
2 level tbsps chopped fresh chives or parsley for garnish

1   Trim and peel carrots. Cut into thin slices.
2   Peel and slice shallot.
3   Put chicken broth into pan. Add sliced carrots and shallot and bring to a boil. Lower heat and simmer until carrots are tender, about 15 minutes.
4   Puree mixture, adding milk.
5   Return purée to pan and thin to desired consistency with milk. It should have consistency of heavy cream or thick vichyssoise. Season.
6   Serve in individual bowls and garnish with chives.

Fusilli with Chicken and Rosemary

1 tablespoon salt
500 g (1 lb) skinless, boneless chicken breasts
4 level tablespoons butter

1 clove garlic, cut in quarters
1 1/2 tsps chopped fresh rosemary, or 1/2 tsp dried
250 -350 ml (8-12 fl oz) light cream or half-and-half
125 g (4 oz) freshly grated Parmesan cheese
Salt
Freshly ground black pepper
500 g (1 lb) fusilli

1   Bring water and 1 tbsp salt to a boil for pasta.
2   Rinse chicken and pat dry with paper towels. Trim and discard all fat and cut breasts into small pieces, about 1 cm (1/2 inch) square.
3   Melt butter and add garlic. Press garlic with back of spoon and rub over surface of pan. Cook until garlic is nut brown, then remove and discard.
4   Turn heat to high and add chicken. Stir constantly to brown all sides quickly, about 1 to 2 minutes.
5   Add rosemary and two thirds of the cream and bring to a simmer.
6   Stir in 60 g (2 oz) of the cheese, taste, then add salt and pepper as needed. Turn off heat and cover.
7   Cook fusilli in boiling water until tender. Drain.
8   When ready to serve, warm sauce. If sauce is too thick, add remaining cream.
9   Serve sauce on pasta at table with extra cheese.

Carrot soup introduces the entrée of fusilli, which is topped with a creamy rosemary, cheese, and chicken sauce.

Menu 3

Mushroom Salad
Fettuccine alla Carbonara
Steamed Broccoli with Lemon Juice and Olive Oil

A classic Roman dish is spaghetti (fettuccine in this version) alla carbonara, which is seasoned with bacon and cheese. Take care to add the beaten eggs, cheese, and cream mixture slowly to the hot pasta; otherwise the eggs cook too quickly and scramble. You can use smoked American bacon – but for an authentic flavour, it is worth buying *pancetta*, a mild unsmoked Italian bacon.

You can serve the broccoli stalks as in the photo below, arranged cartwheel fashion, and insert curled, thinly sliced lemon wedges in the hub.

What to drink
This subtle combination of simple ingredients will match either a white or a red wine. An ideal white would be a dry (*secco*) Orvieto or a California Sauvignon Blanc; an ideal red, a young Chianti.

Steamed broccoli with a delicate lemon and olive oil dressing is a perfect partner for fettuccine all carbonara and a mushroom and watercress salad.

Start-to-Finish Steps
1 Follow pasta recipe steps 1 to 3.
2 Chop parsley and juice lemon for salad recipe and follow salad recipe steps 1 and 2.
3 Grate cheese for pasta recipe and follow pasta recipe steps 4 and 5.
4 Follow broccoli recipe steps 1 and 2. Juice lemon for broccoli recipe and follow broccoli recipe step 3.
5 Follow pasta recipe steps 6 and 7.
6 Follow salad recipe step 3, and serve.
7 Follow pasta recipe step 8, broccoli recipe step 4, and serve both.

Mushroom Salad

250 g (½ lb) fresh mushrooms
100 ml (3 fl oz) olive oil
2 tablespoons fresh lemon juice
Salt and freshly ground black pepper
1 bunch watercress
2 level tablespoons chopped fresh parsley

1 Rinse and trim mushrooms. Do not peel or remove stems. Thinly slice mushrooms.
2 Mix olive oil and lemon juice in bowl and add salt and pepper to taste. Add mushrooms and toss gently.
3 Place watercress on 4 serving plates and top with mushrooms. Sprinkle with chopped parsley.

6 Drain pasta in colander and return it to stockpot. Stir in butter.
7 Add half of the warmed cheese and cream and toss well. Cover.
8 After serving mushroom salad, turn on heat under pasta and eggs, bacon, and remaining cream-and-cheese mixture. Toss well until heated through. If pasta seems dry, add the remaining cream.

Fettuccine alla Carbonara

150 g (5 oz) bacon
2 eggs
250-350 ml (8-12 fl oz) light cream or half-and-half
60 g (2 oz) freshly grated Parmesan cheese
500 g (1 lb) fettuccine
5 level tablespoons butter

1 Bring salted water to a boil in stockpot or kettle.
2 Fry bacon in skillet until crisp. Drain on paper towels; then cut into small pieces.
3 Break eggs into bowl and beat lightly. Set aside.
4 Heat 250 ml (8 fl oz) of the cream and cheese in saucepan, stirring to combine until warmed through.
5 Stir fettuccine into boiling salted water and stir again. It should not cook more than 2 minutes if you are using fresh fettuccine, 5 to 7 minutes if using dried.

Steamed Broccoli with Lemon Juice and Olive Oil

1 bunch broccoli
Salt and freshly ground black pepper
3 tablespoons olive oil
3 tablespoons fresh lemon juice
Lemon wedges for garnish (optional)

1 Wash and trim broccoli. If stalks are large, split lengthwise into 2 or 3 pieces.
2 Place broccoli in vegetable steamer over boiling water and steam until barely tender, 5 to 7 minutes. Remove from heat and put in warm serving bowl.
3 Sprinkle with salt, pepper, olive oil, and lemon juice.
4 Serve with lemon wedges as garnish, if desired.

Sylvia Rosenthal

Menu 1
(*Left*)
Tortellini Salad
Poached Glazed Chicken Breasts

Top-quality fresh ingredients are a prerequisite for any good meal. Sylvia Rosenthal believes that shoppers must learn to reject the second rate and – for the best nutritional value – to take advantage of seasonal crops. She emphasizes that cooking with fresh foods does not mean long hours in the kitchen. By carefully preparing and seasoning fresh ingredients, even a novice cook can produce delicious meals. This New York-based cook book author has long been an advocate of sensible yet elegant dining.

Menu 1 brings together two light but satisfying courses. Meat-filled tortellini, a miniature dumpling, is the main ingredient in the salad. The chicken breasts bake quickly, and, to remain tender, their final fast browning under the grill produces an appetizing glaze.

In Menu 2, Sylvia Rosenthal balances the substantial macaroni entrée with a light mushroom appetizer and a tossed green salad, both seasoned with tangy dressings.

Two Italian favourites, fettuccine and veal scallopini, are the main components of Menu 3. In this recipe, you serve the fettuccine in a rich, creamy Gorgonzola-and-Parmesan cheese sauce. As a contrast, the sautéed veal is dressed with a light sprinkling of lemon and parsley.

Cherry tomatoes border the tortellini salad, dished up on a bed of bright-green lettuce leaves. Garnish the glazed chicken breasts with sprigs of rosemary or parsley. Black-and-white tableware highlights the black olives, cauliflower, and mushrooms in the salad, as well as the sour cream topping on the chicken breasts.

Tortellini Salad
Poached Glazed Chicken Breasts

Various kinds of cooked savoury fillings can be used in tortellini, for example ground meat, cheese, or finely minced cooked vegetables. The filling is spooned onto a circle of dough that is then folded, pinched closed, and tucked into a ring shape. You can buy fresh tortellini in pasta shops or Italian delicatessens. Frozen tortellini are acceptable and better than the dried kind.

Any filled pasta requires gentle handling. Put only three or four at a time in the boiling water. Take care not to overcrowd them. When they are completely cooked, they will float to the top. Cooked tortellini can fall apart very easily, so you must lift them carefully from the pot with a slotted spoon to allow excess water to drain.

Poached chicken breasts are a light yet satisfying accompaniment for pasta salad. Sylvia Rosenthal calls for removing the chicken skin before cooking the breasts – then giving the breasts a last-minute glazing with sour cream for an attractive sheen.

What to drink
Buy a full-bodied, dry white wine – California or Italian Chardonnay or a good French Chablis.

Start-to-Finish Steps
1 Cut cauliflower and broccoli and mince garlic for pasta recipe.
2 Follow pasta recipe step 1.
3 Follow chicken recipe steps 1 to 4. As chicken cooks, follow pasta recipe steps 2 to 7.
4 Follow chicken recipe steps 5 and 6.
5 Follow pasta recipe step 8, and serve with chicken.

Tortellini Salad

250 g (½ lb) meat-filled tortellini, fresh or frozen
250 g (8 oz) cauliflower florets
250 g (8 oz) broccoli florets
4 scallions
60 g (2 oz) black olives, pitted
125 g (½ lb) fresh mushrooms
1 egg yolk
1 tablespoon Dijon mustard
1 small clove garlic, finely minced
2 tablespoons wine vinegar
2 tablespoons dry vermouth
1 teaspoon Worcestershire sauce
125 ml (4 fl oz) vegetable oil
Salt

Freshly ground black pepper
100 ml (3 fl oz) heavy cream
Lettuce leaves for garnish (optional)
500 g (1 lb) cherry tomatoes
Fresh parsley sprigs for garnish (optional)

1 Bring water to a boil in stockpot for pasta and in large saucepan for vegetables.
2 Cook tortellini in boiling water until just done. Fresh will take about 5 minutes, frozen about 6 – do not overcook. Stir occasionally.
3 Drain tortellini, and then transfer to large bowl.
4 Cook cauliflower 3 minutes in saucepan of boiling water; add broccoli and cook 2 minutes more. Drain, and run under cold water to stop cooking.
5 Slice scallions, olives, and mushrooms.
6 Mix egg, mustard, and garlic and beat with whisk. Beat in vinegar, vermouth, and Worcestershire sauce. Add oil, whisking until creamy. Season.
7 Gently fold vegetables into pasta, together with enough dressing to moisten well. Use rubber spatula in order not to break up tortellini or vegetables. Let stand at room temperature until ready to serve.
8 Just before serving, add cream and toss again. Serve on lettuce-lined platter, if desired, with border of cherry tomatoes. Garnish with parsley.

Poached Glazed Chicken Breasts

125 ml (4 fl oz) chicken broth
2 whole skinless, boneless chicken breasts
½ teaspoon salt
Freshly ground black pepper
125 ml (4 fl oz) sour cream
1½ teaspoons crumbled fresh rosemary, or
    ½ teaspoon dried
Fresh parsley or rosemary sprigs for garnish (optional)

1 Preheat oven to 200° (400°F or Mark 6).
2 Heat chicken broth.
3 Wash chicken, pat dry. Trim and discard fat.
4 Place breasts in baking dish. Season and add chicken broth. Cover with foil and place in oven. Bake 20 to 25 mins, until springy to the touch.
5 Transfer breasts to foil-lined grill pan. Spread sour cream over breasts, and sprinkle with rosemary.
6 Place under hot grill and grill 2 or 3 mins, or until cream topping is lightly browned. Remove to serving platter and garnish with parsley or rosemary.

<table>
<tr>
<td>

Menu

2

</td>
<td>

Mushrooms Riviera
Baked Macaroni with Ham and Cheese
Tossed Green Salad

</td>
</tr>
</table>

If you are a mushroom fancier, you may wish to buy 750 g (1½ lbs) of fresh mushrooms for the elegant appetizer in this meal. 500 g (1 lb) of mushrooms, cooks down to provide enough for four people but not enough for second helpings. If you add more mushrooms, be sure to increase the other ingredients to taste but hold back on the salt. For best results, prepare the mushrooms at the last minute.

Macaroni is a general term that describes all hollow pasta, from long spaghetti-like strands to fat tubes. Baked macaroni, an American favourite, originated in Italy centuries ago. This updated version, with its addition of ham, is similar to its Italian ancestor. Although Sylvia Rosenthal calls for boiled ham in this recipe, certainly if you have some good country ham, feel free to use it – and then reduce the amount of salt.

What to drink
You should serve a light, dry red wine, preferably a young one, such as a medium-priced California Merlot or a Saint-Emilion from Bordeax. Saint-Emilion is a blend of Merlot and other grapes to make a dry, soft wine that harmonizes well with sauces and foods of complex texture and varied flavours.

Start-to-Finish Steps
1 Grate cheese for pasta recipe. Mince garlic for salad recipe.
2 Follow pasta recipe steps 1 and 2.
3 Follow salad recipe steps 1 and 2.
4 Follow pasta recipe steps 3 to 10.
5 Trim and toast bread and cut into triangles for mushroom recipe. Crush anchovies, chop parsley, and juice lemon for mushroom recipe.
6 Follow mushroom recipe steps 1 to 4.
7 Follow salad recipe steps 3 to 5 and mushroom recipe step 5, and serve.

This informal family meal features an appetizingly crusty baked macaroni combined with ham and cheese, sautéed mushrooms served on toast triangles, and a light salad of lettuce and avocado slices.

Mushrooms Riviera

500 g (1 lb) fresh mushrooms
3 level tablespoons butter
1 clove garlic
4 anchovy fillets, crushed
3 level tablespoons chopped fresh parsley
2 tablespoons lemon juice
Salt
Freshly ground black pepper
2 slices bread, crusts trimmed, toasted, and cut into
    triangles

1 Wipe mushrooms clean and trim stem ends. Thinly slice caps and stems.
2 Melt butter in skillet and add garlic. Remove and discard garlic when browned.
3 Add mushrooms and cook over moderately high heat, stirring often. After about 5 minutes, there will be fair amount of mushroom liquid. Spoon a few tablespoons of the liquid into the anchovies, making thick paste. Add paste to mushrooms, blending well. Cook 5 minutes more, or until liquid is absorbed.
4 Add parsley and lemon juice to mushrooms and toss lightly. Taste and correct seasonings. Anchovies will probably make additional salt unnecessary.
5 Place each portion of mushrooms on toast triangle and serve at once.

Baked Macaroni with Ham and Cheese

250 g ($^1/_2$ lb) short tubular macaroni, such as ziti
6 level tablespoons butter
3 level tablespoons flour
625 ml (1$^1/_4$ pts) milk
250 g (8 oz) grated strong mature Cheddar cheese
Salt
Freshly ground black pepper
250 g ($^1/_2$ lb) cooked ham, sliced 5 mm ($^1/_4$ inch) thick
Paprika

1 Bring water to a boil for pasta in stockpot.
2 Preheat oven to 190°C (375°F or Mark 5).
3 Butter casserole or soufflé dish.
4 Salt water and add macaroni to rapidly boiling water and cook only until slightly tender, 6 to 7 minutes. Pasta will cook further in oven, so it should be slightly underdone.
5 In saucepan, heat two thirds of the butter and stir in flour. Cook over medium heat, stirring, until bubbly – about 3 minutes.
6 Remove pan from heat and vigorously stir in milk to blend well. Return pan to heat and stir and cook until sauce has thickened. Add 3 level tablespoons of the grated cheese and stir until melted. Add salt and pepper to taste.
7 Cut ham slices into 5 mm ($^1/_4$ inch) cubes.
8 Place colander in sink and drain cooked macaroni. Shake colander to get rid of excess water. Return macaroni to pot and toss with cream sauce and ham.
9 Arrange layer of the macaroni in casserole; cover with generous dusting of paprika and layer of the shredded cheese. Continue layering until all are used, ending with cheese. You will find 3 layers about right. Dot top with the remaining butter.
10 Bake 25 to 30 minutes, or until bubbling.

Tossed Green Salad

1 head leaf lettuce, red tipped if available
$^1/_2$ head cos
1 small ripe avocado
2 tablespoons wine vinegar
1 tablespoon Dijon mustard
1 clove garlic, minced
6 tablespoons olive oil
Salt
Freshly ground black pepper

1 Core lettuces and separate leaves. Rinse greens, and dry them well in salad spinner or with paper towels.
2 Break greens into bite-size pieces and place in salad bowl. There will be approximately 250 g (8 oz) torn salad greens. Chill.
3 Cut avocado in half, peel, and remove pit. Slice into thin strips or cubes.
4 Combine vinegar, mustard, and garlic in mixing bowl. Blend with whisk and add oil slowly. Season with salt and pepper to taste.
5 Toss greens and avocado with dressing.

<table>
<tr><td>

Menu

3

</td><td>

Fettuccine with Gorgonzola Sauce
Veal Scallopini with Lemon and Parsley
Carrots and Peas with Dill

</td></tr>
</table>

The main course for this meal includes fettuccine, pasta shaped like slender ribbons. Fettuccine popularly is served with Parmesan cheese, but this recipe calls for both Parmesan and Gorgonzola, a sharp-tasting blue cheese. It is delicious combined with pasta or fresh fruit, crumbled into salad dressings, or grilled on toast. The green of the spinach fettuccine – which this recipe calls for – makes a pretty colour contrast with the cheese, but if the spinach fettuccine is not available, you can use ordinary egg fettuccine without changing the taste of the dish. Either the fresh or the dried fettuccine will work well.

Most veal available today comes from older grain-fed calves. The top-quality very young veal may be available from specialized outlets. Choose firm cutlets, velvety in texture, and ivory-pink in colour. Ask your butcher to pound the cutlets thin for scallopini, or you may wish to do this at home. Place the meat slices

Garnish the veal with lemon slices and parsley. For visual appeal, arrange the carrots and peas separately in a tureen.

on a wooden board; then with a meat pounder or mallet, gently flatten and enlarge each slice until it is twice its original size. To prevent its tearing, keep the meat slightly moistened while pounding. You can also place the meat between two sheets of waxed paper. Beacause the veal is expensive, you may decide to substitute the more economical boned chicken or turkey breasts. Treat them exactly as you would veal.

What to drink

The veal and pasta dishes in this menu will be a good match for either red or white wines. If you want white, get a dry California Riesling. For a red, choose a young Barbera from California or from Italy.

Start-to-Finish Steps

1. Juice lemon and chop dill for carrot recipe. Slice and juice lemon and chop parsley for veal recipe. Grate Parmesan cheese for pasta recipe.
2. Follow pasta recipe step 1. As water comes to a boil, follow carrot recipe steps 1 and 2.
3. Follow veal recipe steps 1 to 4.
4. Follow pasta recipe step 2.
5. Follow carrot recipe step 3.
6. Follow pasta recipe steps 3 and 4.
7. Follow veal recipe steps 5 to 8.
8. Follow pasta recipe step 5, and serve with veal and glazed carrots and peas.

Fettuccine with Gorgonzola Sauce

Salt
125 g (¹/₄ lb) Gorgonzola cheese
3 level tablespoons butter
60 ml (2 fl oz) milk
500 g (1 lb) spinach fettuccine
175 ml (6 fl oz) heavy cream
125 g (4 oz) freshly grated Parmesan cheese

1. Bring water to a boil for pasta in stockpot.
2. In enamel-lined baking pan, or gratin pan that can be brought to table, mash Gorgonzola cheese over low heat and stir in butter and milk. Cook, stirring, until sauce becomes thick and creamy – about 1 minute. Remove from heat and set aside.
3. When water is boiling, add 2 tablespoons salt and fettuccine. Cover pot just until water comes back to a boil; then remove lid. Fresh pasta will cook in 1 to 3 minutes; dry pasta in about 8 minutes. Be certain to undercook because fettucine will cook a bit more in pan. Fish out a strand to taste for readiness.

4. Just before removing pasta from water, turn heat under sauce to low and stir in cream.
5. Place colander in sink and drain pasta. Give colander good shake to get rid of all water. Transfer pasta to pan with sauce, add 60 g (2 oz) of the grated cheese, and toss together. Serve immediately with a bowl of the remaining grated Parmesan cheese on side.

Veal Scallopini with Lemon and Parsley

3 tablespoons vegetable oil
4 level tablespoons butter
60 g (2 oz) flour
500g (1 lb) veal scallopini, thinly sliced and pounded thin
¹/₂ teaspoon salt
Pepper
Juice of 1 lemon, plus 1 lemon thinly sliced
3 level tablespoons chopped fresh parsley

1. Preheat oven to SLOW.
2. Heat oil and three quarters of the butter in skillet or sauté pan over medium-high heat.
3. Spread flour on waxed paper and dip both sides of veal slices in it, shaking off excess. Dip slices in flour only when you are ready to sauté them to avoid sogginess.
4. Place scallopini in hot fat – as many as will fit comfortably in single layer without crowding. Cook until brown on 1 side, turn, and brown other side. If thin enough, they will need about 2 minutes per side. When done, sprinkle lightly with salt and pepper and transfer to warm platter. Keep

warm in oven. Continue this process until all are cooked. (If fat has burned, pour it off and add additional butter to pan.)

5 Remove skillet from heat and add lemon juice, stirring and scraping up browned bits on bottom of pan.

6 Swirl in the remaining butter and stir in chopped parsley.

7 Just before serving, return cooked scallopini to sauce and heat briefly, just enough to warm through.

8 Transfer to warm platter; pour extra sauce over meat and top each scallopini with lemon slices.

Carrots and Peas with Dill

350 g (12 oz) package finger carrots, or 6 to 7 large
  carrots
2 level tablespoons butter
1¹/₂ teaspoons sugar
¹/₂ teaspoon salt
1 tablespoon lemon juice
175 ml (6 fl oz) water
300 g (10 oz) package frozen peas, defrosted
1 tablespoon chopped fresh dill, or 1 teaspoon dried

1 Trim and scrape carrots. Leave whole, or thinly slice if using large ones.

2 Place carrots, butter, sugar, salt, and lemon juice in saucepan. Add 175 ml (6 fl oz) boiling water. Cook over high heat until water returns to a lively boil. Lower heat, cover, and cook 10 minutes, or until carrots are slightly tender.

3 Uncover saucepan, add peas, and continue cooking until water has evaporated and carrots and peas are lightly glazed. Sprinkle with dill. Keep warm in oven until ready to serve.

Added touch
Homemade sherbet and fresh pineapple slices make a refreshing dessert.

Pineapple Slices with Lemon Sherbet

750 ml (1¹/₂ pts) water
350 g (12 oz) sugar
125 ml (4 fl oz) lemon juice
Grated rind of 1 lemon
2 egg whites, at room temperature
4 slices fresh pineapple, peeled and cored
60 ml (2 fl oz) crème de menthe (optional)

1 Chill metal bowl in freezer. Combine water and sugar in saucepan; bring to a boil over moderate heat and boil 5 minutes. Cool.

2 When cool, add lemon juice and grated rind.

3 Pour into 2 refrigerator trays, cover trays with plastic wrap, and place in freezer.

4 Beat egg whites until stiff.

5 When mixture in refrigerator is frozen to mushy consistency, about 1 hour, transfer to cold metal bowl and quickly beat with electric or rotary beater until smooth.

6 Fold in beaten egg whites. Pour into refrigerator trays, cover, and freeze again.

7 Remove mixture to cold bowl and quickly beat again until smooth.

8 Return to trays, cover, and freeze until firm, about 2 hours.

9 Remove sherbet from freezer to refrigerator 20 to 30 minutes before serving time, to allow it to soften a little.

10 To serve, place slice of pineapple on dessert plate. Top pineapple with scoop of sherbet and drizzle a bit of crème de menthe over sherbet.

Leftover suggestion
Leftover cooked pasta, depending on its shape, can be incorporated into a variety of new dishes, such as a salad or an omelette. This spaghetti omelette is so delicious you may consider cooking the spaghetti especially for this dish.

Spaghetti Omelette

4 eggs
30 g (1 oz) freshly grated Parmesan cheese
2 level tablespoons chopped fresh parsley
Salt
Freshly ground black pepper
250 g (8 oz) leftover cooked spaghetti
2 tablespoons olive oil
2 level tablespoons butter
500 ml (1 pt) tomato sauce (optional)

1 Beat eggs lightly and stir in cheese, parsley, salt, and pepper. Add to spaghetti and mix well.

2 Heat oil and butter in large skillet. Spread spaghetti over bottom of pan and cook over medium heat 3 to 4 minutes, or until underside has lightly golden crust.

3 Invert onto plate and then slide it back into pan. Cook other side until slightly crusty. Serve with hot tomato sauce, if desired. Cut into wedges to serve.

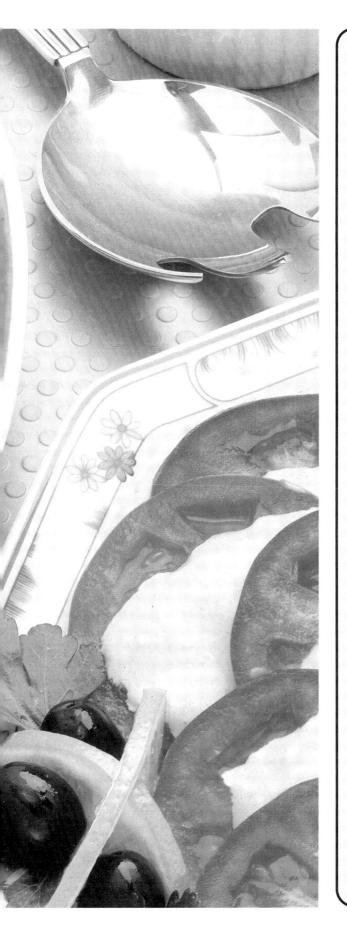

Diane Darrow and Tom Maresca

Menu 1
(left)
Sliced Tomatoes with Tuna Sauce
Spaghetti with Peppers, Aubergine,
and Tomatoes

Diane Darrow and Tom Maresca, a husband-wife team living in New York City, favour the Italian custom of eating several small courses rather than building their meal around one large main course. Their at-home suppers may consist of only an antipasto and pasta or only a pasta and a salad and perhaps a loaf of Italian Bread. Their desserts are usually seasonal fruits served with a platter of cheese – also an Italian custom.

The Darrow-Maresca approach to dining is reflected in their menus, which progress through several balanced courses, all suitable for informal meals. Menu 2, an elegant party dinner, is the only exception, with its unusual first course of veal tartare and a delicate second course capelli d'angelo, or 'angel's hair' pasta. Menu 1 is an economical meatless meal, and its pasta course is spaghetti, teamed here with peppers, aubergines, and tomatoes. These vegetables are simmered together and seasoned with garlic, capers, anchovies, and a grating of Parmesan cheese. Menu 3, which features rigatoni dressed with a sauce of mushrooms and chicken livers, does not call for any seasonal produce, so you can serve it at any time of year.

You can serve the antipasto dish of sliced tomatoes and tuna sauce – garnished with black olives, Italian parsley, and crossed lemon slices – while you heat a loaf of Italian bread. Then bring on the main course of spaghetti with peppers, aubergine, and tomatoes, served in a rimmed platter, and the hot bread. Pass the freshly grated Parmesan separately.

Sliced Tomatoes with Tuna Sauce
Spaghetti with Peppers, Aubergines, and Tomatoes

This economical meatless summer menu features two seasonal favourites – ripe tomatoes and aubergines. The first course of tomatoes in tuna sauce is a variation of *vitello tonnato*, a classic dish that features thinly sliced veal steeped in a creamy tuna and anchovy-based sauce. By substituting sliced tomatoes for veal, Diane Darrow and Tom Maresca have created something much lighter. If vine-ripened tomatoes are not in season, they suggest that you use slices of peeled and thinly sliced raw celery root, roasted and peeled green peppers, or raw crisp courgette. To crisp fresh courgettes, place whole courgettes in a bowl of iced water in the refrigerator early in the morning and leave them to chill for the day. At serving time, remove the courgettes from the water, dry them thoroughly, and slice thinly. For a richer tuna flavour, buy canned Italian tuna packed in olive oil.

Like many Italian recipes, this one calls for fresh basil, generally available only in the summer season. Rather then using dried basil, which does not have the same mild minty flavour, they recommend that you freeze batches of fresh basil for year-round use.

The first course should be garnished with imported Moroccan or Sicilian olives. If you cannot find them, substitute any kind of oil-cured ripe olive. A decorative trick for garnishing this dish – and one that is simple to do – is to slice and arrange the lemons in the following manner. Take centre-cut, round lemon slices and cut them in half. Notch the centre of one half through the flesh and almost through the rind. Slip uncut halves into the notches' so the pieces will stand up at right angles forming an arched X. Add an olive or a sprig of parsley.

The spaghetti recipe is a variation of a traditional Sicilian dish. If possible, buy small Italian or Oriental aubergines, about the length of a finger, which are sweeter and have fewer seeds than the larger ones.

What to drink
Summer flavours like these call for a cold white wine with some body and depth. Try an Italian Greco di Tufo or a Cortese, or a California sauvignon or Fumé Blanc. Marsala – sweet or dry – goes well with the fruit dessert.

Start-to-Finish Steps
1   Juice 2 lemons and slice third lemon for garnish, if desired, for tomato recipe. Grate cheese and chop 2 teaspoons basil for pasta recipe. Measure out 175 g (6 oz) of the canned tomatoes with their juice for pasta recipe.
2   Follow pasta recipe steps 1 to 5. When water comes to a boil, preheat oven to 180°C (350°F or Mark 4).
3   Follow pasta recipe step 6.
4   Follow tomato recipe steps 1 to 3.
5   Follow pasta recipe steps 7 and 8. Warm bread in oven.
6   Follow tomato recipe steps 4 to 6.
7   Follow pasta recipe steps 9 and 10. Serve with tomatoes.

Sliced Tomatoes with Tuna sauce

1 egg
2 tablespoons lemon juice
1 teaspoon Dijon mustard
$^1/_8$ teaspoon salt
250 ml (8 fl oz) olive oil
200 g (7 oz) can dark-meat tuna packed in olive oil
1 anchovy fillet
2 level tablespoons capers
750 g (1$^1/_2$ lbs) ripe tomatoes
8 Sicilian or Moroccan black olives, not brine packed
Lemon slices for garnish (optional)
1 loaf Italian or French bread

Put egg, 1 tablespoon of the lemon juice, mustard, and salt into bowl of blender or food processor. Process 1 minute with metal blade.

2 With machine running, add 60 ml (2 fl oz) of the olive oil in stream of droplets. Then gradually add the remaining oil, anchovy, the remaining 1 tablespoon of lemon juice, and capers. Blend until sauce is smooth.

3 Add tuna and all its oil, anchovy, the remaining 1 tablespoon of lemon juice, and capers. Blend until sauce is smooth.

4 Slice tomatoes 5 mm (^{1}/$_4$ inch) thick.

5 Choose serving platter large enough to hold all tomato slices in 1 or 2 layers with minimal overlap. Spread platter with thin layer of the tuna sauce. Place tomato slices on sauce and spoon the remaining sauce over. Refrigerate until ready to serve.

6 At serving time, garnish platter with black olives and slices of lemon, as desired. Serve with loaf of fresh Italian or French bread, warmed 5 minutes in 180°C (350°F or Mark 4) oven.

Spaghetti with Peppers, Aubergines, and Tomatoes

250 g (^{1}/$_2$ lb) aubergines
2 anchovy fillets
2 teaspoons capers
5 tablespoons olive oil
2 large cloves garlic, unpeeled
2 large red or yellow bell peppers (about 350 g (^{3}/$_4$ lb))
2 teaspoons chopped fresh basil, or 2 teaspoons frozen
175 g (6 oz) canned Italian plum tomatoes, coarsely chopped, with juices
Salt
Freshly ground black pepper
500g (1 lb) spaghetti
100 g (3 oz) freshly grated Parmesan cheese

1 Peel aubergines and chop into 1 cm (^{1}/$_2$ inch) pieces.

2 Rinse salt from anchovy fillets, pat dry, and cut each into 2 or 3 pieces. Rinse and drain capers. Set aside.

3 Warm olive oil in non-aluminium sauté pan or casserole. Add aubergines, anchovies, and unpeeled garlic cloves. Sauté over moderate heat, stirring occasionally, 5 to 8 minutes, or until aubergines are soft.

4 Wash peppers, slice in half, and remove seeds and membranes. Cut crosswise into 5 mm (^{1}/$_4$ inch) strips. Roughly chop tomatoes.

5 Bring stockpot of water to a boil for pasta. Add 2 tablespoons salt and bring to a rolling boil.

6 When aubergines are soft, add peppers, tomatoes, capers, and basil to sauté pan. Stir well. Bring to a simmer, cover, and cook over medium heat, stirring occasionally, 12 to 15 minutes, or until peppers are tender.

7 Meanwhile, cook spaghetti in boiling water until *al dente*.

8 Remove garlic cloves from sauce and discard. Taste for seasoning and add salt, if necessary, add generous amount of pepper. Set sauce aside until pasta is ready.

9 Drain spaghetti in colander and then return it to stockpot. Add half of the sauce and toss to coat thoroughly; then add half of the cheese and toss again. Keep warm in turned-off oven while serving first course.

10 When ready to serve, heat the remaining sauce and add to spaghetti, tossing well. Serve the remaining cheese at table.

Added touch

For a light, elegant dessert for this meal, use sweet fresh peaches. Slice them in half and fill with crumbled *amaretti* – Italian macaroons – brandy, and unsweetened cocoa, all of which are complementary flavours for summer-ripe peaches.

Baked Stuffed Peaches

4 large firm ripe freestone peaches
100 g (3 oz) *amaretti* cookies (about 14)
1^1/$_2$ level tablespoons sugar
1^1/$_2$ teaspoons unsweetened cocoa
1 teaspoon brandy
1 level tablespoon butter

1 Preheat oven to 180°C (350°F or Mark 4).

2 Wash and dry peaches, but do not peel. Cut in half and remove stones. With teaspoon, scoop out some of the pulp to enlarge cavities, but leave wall about 1 cm (^{1}/$_2$ inch) thick all around.

3 Mince removed pulp and place in small bowl. Crumble *amaretti* cookies into bowl, and stir into peach pulp along with sugar, cocoa, and brandy. Stuff peaches with mixture.

4 Butter 4 individual oblong gratin dishes, and set 2 stuffed peach halves in each. Bake 30 minutes. Serve hot, warm, or at room temperature.

Veal Tartare
Capelli d'Angelo with Asparagus Sauce

Asparagus and mushrooms tossed with prosciutto and served on a bed of slender pasta follow the first course of veal tartare.

For veal tartare, you must use good-quality lean veal, preferably minced at the very last moment. The best cuts of veal for this recipe come from the leg or the more economical shoulder cut. If you have a food processor or mincer, mince the veal at home just before serving the meal. Otherwise, have it minced at the meat counter the same day you serve it. Be sure that the mincing equipment is very clean in either case. If the butcher is doing the mincing, tell him you intend to serve the meat raw. Keep the veal well chilled until you use it and do not save any leftovers, since minced raw meat spoils quickly. (Note: most doctors now advise pregnant women to eat no raw meat at all.) The lemon juice, which you sprinkle over the veal, does all the 'cooking' necessary for the raw meat dish.

The pasta is a springtime dish since it features fresh asparagus. Capelli d'angelo, or 'angel's hair,' is the slenderest of all Italian pastas. Because it cooks quickly, you must watch it carefully. Fresh angel hair pasta will cook in just under one minute, the dried in one to two minutes.

What to drink
A full-bodied white wine or a light red is the right wine to accompany this elegant meal: either a good-quality California Chardonnay or an Italian Cabernet would be best. In either case, the younger the better.

Start-to-Finish Steps
1 Grate cheese for pasta and veal recipes.
2 Follow pasta recipe steps 1 to 4.
3 Mince onion and parsley for veal recipe. Juice lemons for veal recipe.
4 Follow veal recipe steps 1 to 4. Refrigerate.
5 Follow pasta recipe steps 5 to 9.
6 Follow veal recipe steps 5 and 6 and serve.
7 Follow pasta recipe step 10 and serve.

Veal Tartare

500 g (1 lb) lean veal shoulder or tenderloin
2 teaspoons salt
3 tablespoons lemon juice
2 tablespoons finely minced onion
$1/2$ teaspoon freshly ground black pepper
125 ml (4 fl oz) olive oil
125 g ($1/4$ lb) fresh mushrooms
30 g (1 oz) freshly grated Parmesan cheese
Minced parsley and/or capers for garnish (optional)
3 slices firm white bread, crusts trimmed, cut into
    triangles

1   Carefully trim veal and discard any sinew and fat.
2   In bowl, dissolve salt in lemon juice. Add onion,
    pepper, and olive oil. Mix well.
3   Slice mushrooms very thin. In bowl, toss with 3
    tablespoons of the dressing from step 2.
4   Mince veal in food processor or mincer. Add
    cheese and mix in well. Pour in dressing and
    process briefly until mixed.
5   Mound veal on individual plates. Surround with
    decorative ring of mushroom slices and garnish
    with parsley and/or capers, as desired.
6   Just before serving, toast bread triangles. Serve
    with veal and pass pepper mill at table.

Capelli d'Angelo with Asparagus Sauce

500 g (1 lb) fresh asparagus
250 g ($1/2$ lb) fresh mushrooms
3 tablespoons olive oil
Salt
3 level tablespoons plus 2 teaspoons butter
Freshly ground black pepper
2 teaspoons chopped fresh thyme, or $1/2$ teaspoon
    dried
2 level tablespoons flour
250 ml (8 fl oz) chicken or beef broth
2 eggs
125 g (4 oz) freshly grated Parmesan cheese
2 slices prosciutto (about 30 g (1 oz))
500 g (1 lb) capelli d'angelo

1   Preheat oven to SLOW.
2   Bring water to a boil in stockpot for pasta. Also
    bring saucepan of water to boil for asparagus.
3   Snap off and discard tough bottoms of asparagus.
    Wash spears and cut into $2^1/2$ cm (1 inch) lengths.
    Blanch in boiling water 1 minute, then run under
cold water to stop cooking. Separate tips from
stalks, and set both parts aside.
4   Wipe mushrooms and cut into 5 mm ($1/4$ inch)
    slices.
5   Heat olive oil in large skillet. Add mushrooms and
    sauté over high heat about 1 minute, stirring
    constantly, until they take up all oil. Turn heat to
    low, sprinkle mushrooms lightly with salt, and
    continue cooking – stirring – until they begin to
    exude juices, about 1 more minute. Turn heat to
    medium-high, and cook about 1 minute more,
    stirring, until slices are tender.
6   Add 3 level tablespoons of the butter to saucepan
    and, when melted, add cut-up asparagus stalks
    (not tips) and thyme. Add salt and pepper to taste
    and sauté over moderate heat 3 to 4 minutes,
    depending on thickness of asparagus. Sprinkle
    flour over vegetables, and stir 1 minute. Add
    broth, bring to a boil, and simmer 1 minute. Cover
    sauce and set aside until ready to use.
7   In bowl, mix eggs, cheese, $1/2$ teaspoon salt, and
    $1/2$ teaspoon pepper.
8   Cut prosciutto slices into 5 mm ($1/4$ inch) strips and
    warm together with asparagus tips in small skillet
    with the remaining 2 teaspoons of the butter.
    Keep warm in turned -off oven.
9   Plunge capelli d'angelo into boiling water and
    watch it very carefully – it cooks quickly. When *al
    dente*, drain well, turn back into stockpot, and
    toss thoroughly with half of the asparagus sauce.
    Keep warm in turned-off oven.
10 When ready to serve, toss with egg-and-cheese
    mixture and the remaining asparagus sauce. Turn
    into warm serving bowl and scatter prosciutto and
    asparagus tips over top.

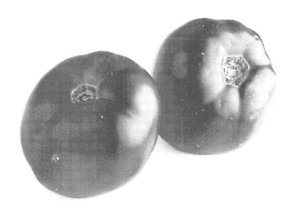

Mozzarella Tart
Rigatoni with Mushroom and Chicken Liver Sauce
Spinach and Chicory Salad

This is an economical family meal, suitable for any time of year. The rigatoni dish, of Neapolitan origins, takes advantage of the affinity between chicken livers and mushrooms. The two are sautéed together, then simmered in a light tomato sauce. A large tubular pasta such as rigatoni is a logical choice for this thick, chunky sauce.

The mozzarella tart, which may sound complicated, is actually a quick-to-assemble dish. Treat the bread slices as if you were making French toast, and once they have soaked up the egg dip, layer the cheese over the bread.

What to drink

For this meal you will need a hearty wine with some degree of complexity in its flavour: a Barbera or Dolcetto from the Piedmont in northern Italy would be fine. You can also try a full-bodied Zinfandel from California. If you decide to make the dessert, save some Marsala to sip after dessert along with your coffee.

Start-to-Finish Steps

1   Chop herbs for pasta recipe. Juice lemon for salad.
2   Follow pasta recipe steps 1 to 7. As water comes

Chunky rigatoni, served with a mushroom and chicken liver sauce, accompanies the mozzarella tart appetizer. A mixed green salad, a brightly coloured table setting, and an ivy plant centrepiece make the meal even more appealing.

to a boil and sauce simmers, follow tart recipe steps 1 to 6. As tart bakes, follow pasta recipe step 8 and salad recipe step 1.

3 Serve mozzarella tart.
4 Follow pasta recipe step 9.
5 Follow salad recipe step 2, and serve with pasta.

Mozzarella Tart

2 level tablespoons butter, softened
1 egg yolk
60 ml (2 fl oz) milk
8 anchovy fillets
8 slices French or Italian bread, about 1 cm (¹/₂ inch) thick (crusts trimmed, if desired)
250 g (¹/₂ lb) mozzarella cheese
1 teaspoon fennel seeds or dried oregano, or ¹/₂ teaspoon each
2 level tablespoons freshly grated Parmesan cheese

1 Preheat oven to 200°C (400°F or Mark 6).
2 Generously grease baking dish.
3 Put egg yolk, milk, and anchovy fillets into blender and blend until smooth, or mash anchovy with egg yolk in small bowl and beat in milk with whisk.
4 Arrange bread slices in 1 layer in baking dish and moisten each slice with 1¹/₂ tablespoons of the blended liquid. Try not to let mixture spill over onto bottom of pan. If bread is reluctant to take up liquid, pierce it here and there with fork to hasten absorption. You can dip bread slices into blended liquid, but you do not want them too soggy.
5 Cut mozzarella into thin slices and lay evenly over bread. Sprinkle fennel or oregano over top; or put fennel on half of the slices and oregano on the other half. Sprinkle Parmesan evenly over all.
6 Bake uncovered 20 minutes, or until cheese is bubbly and just starting to brown on top. Let sit 5 minutes before serving.

Rigatoni with Mushroom and Chicken Liver Sauce

100 g (3 oz) chopped onions
60 g (2 oz) prosciutto fat, or fat from any good cured
    ham
250 g (½ lb) fresh mushrooms
4 slices prosciutto (about 60 g (2 oz))
250 g (½ lb) chicken livers
175 g (6 oz) butter
250 ml (8 fl oz) dry red wine
350 g (12 oz) canned Italian plum tomatoes, drained
Freshly ground black pepper
¾ teaspoon chopped fresh basil, or ¾ teaspoon
    frozen
Salt
500g (1 lb) rigatoni
60 g (2 oz) freshly grated Parmesan cheese
¾ teaspoon chopped fresh parsley for garnish
    (optional)

1   Finely chop onion together with prosciutto fat.
2   Wipe mushrooms and cut into thin slices. Cut prosciutto into 5 mm (¼ inch) strips.
3   Trim chicken livers, removing and discarding any bits of fat or membrane, and cut each into pieces no larger than 2½ cm (1 inch).
4   Put salted water on to boil for pasta in stockpot.
5   Set casserole over low heat. Melt one third of the butter and sauté onion and prosciutto fat until fat is rendered and onion is translucent – about 2 minutes. Add mushrooms and chopped prosciutto and continue to simmer, stirring often, another 2 minutes. Add livers and sauté, stirring 1 minute, or until they have just lost raw red colour.
6   Raise heat, pour in wine, and cook, stirring, until wine is completely evaporated. Set food mill fitted with medium-size blade over casserole, and mill in tomatoes. Alternatively, mash tomatoes thoroughly with a fork before adding to casserole. Add generous amount of pepper. If using frozen basil, add it to sauce now.
7   Bring sauce to a boil, reduce heat to maintain gentle simmer, and cook, covered, 15 to 20 minutes, or until tomatoes have completely dissolved and sauce is slightly thickened. Taste for salt. If prosciutto is very salty, none may be needed.
8   Meanwhile, cook rigatoni in boiling water until *al dente*, 15 to 18 minutes. Drain pasta in colander and return to stockpot. Toss with the remaining butter, cut into several pieces. Add grated Parmesan cheese and half of the sauce, tossing well after each. Keep warm in turned-off oven.
9   When ready to serve, add the remaining sauce and toss well. Turn into large warm serving bowl and sprinkle chopped fresh basil over top. If you used frozen basil in sauce, garnish with chopped parsley, if desired.

Spinach and Chicory Salad

175 g (6 oz) crisp fresh spinach
175 g (6 oz) chicory
Scant ¼ teaspoon salt
2 teaspoons lemon juice
2 to 3 tablespoons olive oil

1   Remove and discard spinach stems. Wash spinach and chicory carefully; drain and spin dry. Tear leaves into bite-size pieces and put in large salad bowl.
2   At serving time, put salt and lemon juice into bowl of salad serving spoon. Stir with salad serving fork to dissolve salt. Sprinkle this over greens, and then sprinkle olive oil over. Toss thoroughly.

Added touch

Zabaglione, a rich egg custard, is a favourite Italian dessert that you can serve at room temperature or chilled. Its classic flavouring is Marsala, a sweetish Italian dessert wine. You can also make this dessert with Madeira.

Zabaglione

3 egg yolks
3 level tablespoons sugar
100 ml (3 fl oz) dry Marsala

1   Put yolks and sugar in top of double boiler but not over water. With whisk or hand-held electric mixer, whip until they become pale cream colour.
2   Set double-boiler top over simmering water, add Marsala, and continue beating, about 3 minutes, until cream foams and mounds into smooth custard.
3   Scoop into individual serving dishes and serve at once, preferably with crisp nut cookies.

Added touch

If you have more than an hour to spend making this meal, try this baked banana confection. It has an Oriental flavour that comes from the chopped crystallized ginger.

Baked Bananas with Meringue Topping

4 to 6 firm bananas
2 tablespoons lemon juice
3 level tablespoons crystallized ginger, finely chopped
3 egg whites, at room temperature
Pinch of salt
$1/4$ teaspoon cream of tartar
6 level tablespoons sugar
1 teaspoon vanilla extract

1   Preheat oven to 190°C (375°F or Mark 5). Lightly grease baking sheet.
2   Peel bananas and cut in half lengthwise. Arrange on baking sheet with 2 halves side by side, cut side down, leaving space between pairs. Sprinkle with lemon juice, and dot with ginger.
3   In medium-size bowl, beat egg whites until foamy. Add salt and cream of tartar and beat until soft peaks form. Add sugar slowly, beating costantly, until meringue stands in stiff, shiny peaks, beat in vanilla.
4   With pastry tube or 2 spoons, spread meringue on surfaces of banana halves, making a swirl pattern with back of spoon.
5   Bake 15 to 20 minutes, or until meringue is lightly browned. Remove from baking sheet with metal turner and serve while warm.

Jane Salzfass Freiman

Menu 1
(left)
Spaghettini with Yogurt Pesto
Grilled Salmon Fillets with Chives
in Lemon Butter Sauce
Sliced Tomato and Goat Cheese Salad

Homemade pasta has its own attributes, but Jane Salzfass Freiman believes that dried pasta is a more adaptable, sturdier ingredient for such dishes as salads. She feels that a basic accomplishment for any cook – and one that is easy to master – is to learn how to prepare commercial dried pasta. She recommends choosing a dried pasta – and, of course, any fine pasta – with a smooth texture and a uniform golden colour from the semolina flour.

Because of her classic European and American cooking training, Jane Salzfass Freiman promotes – through her cooking classes and syndicated food column – the use of fresh, natural ingredients. Additionally, she creates recipes that stress strong, direct flavours, such as you find in Menu 1 and Menu 3. Menu 1, a light summery meal, is accented by the pesto, or basil paste – unusual in this version because the base of the pesto is yogurt rather than the traditional oil-and-cheese enrichment. The goat cheese, now a popular cheese, in the tomato salad also fortifies this dish. Menu 3, a simple but festive meal, is sparked by the pungent curry that seasons the roasted chicken.

The pasta salad in Menu 2 features fresh asparagus, which has a short season in spring. At other times of the year, you can use alternative fresh produce instead, such as broccoli or Chinese snow peas.

Grilled salmon fillets, tomato and goat cheese salad, and spaghettini with its green pesto dressing makes an impressive, light meal – a perfect lunch for guests. Garnish the goat cheese slices with a spoonful of chopped parsley; at the last minute, pour the vinaigrette around the tomato slices. To fill out the meal, you might want to add some warm French bread.

Spaghettini with Yogurt Pesto
Grilled Salmon Fillets with Chives in Lemon Butter Sauce
Sliced Tomato and Goat Cheese Salad

The green-and-white first course of spaghettini with yogurt pesto introduces this warm-weather meal. Pesto, a traditional Italian sauce, contains fresh basil ground to a paste with various other ingredients, such as olive oil, pine nuts, garlic, and Parmesan cheese – and, in this version, yogurt. To achieve an authentic pesto flavour, you must use only fresh basil.

Salmon is a fish prized for its delicate flavour and rich, firm flesh. It is widely available in fishmongers. Farmed salmon is less expensive than its wild counterparts, but wild salmon is considered superior in texture and taste. If you do not have top-of-the-stove grill, use a heavy iron skillet with a ridged bottom or a heavy cast-iron or cast-aluminium grill with a corrugated cooking surface. The ridged surface brands the food with the familiar grill stripes and keeps the food out of the fat.

You may wish to alter the salmon recipe by baking rather than grilling the fish. If so, brush the fillets with Dijon mustard, then sprinkle them with bread crumbs.

Goat cheese, or *chèvre* in French, is the key ingredient in the tomato salad. Its pronounced, salty taste goes especially well with either fresh fruit or ripe tomatoes. You can substitute mozzarella for the goat cheese if you prefer.

What to drink
The bright and summery but opulent flavours here need a white wine of some fullness – a medium-priced California Chardonnay or a more delicate New York State Chardonnay.

Start-to-Finish Steps
1 Mince parsley for salad recipe and squeeze lemon for salad recipe.
2 Follow salmon recipe steps 1 to 4.
3 Follow pasta recipe steps 1 to 3.
4 Follow salad recipe steps 1 to 4.
5 Follow salmon recipe step 5.
6 Follow pasta recipe step 4. As pasta cooks, follow salmon recipe step 6.
7 Follow pasta recipe steps 5 and 6. Follow salmon recipe step 7 and salad recipe step 5. Serve.

Spaghettini with Yogurt Pesto

2 medium cloves garlic
3 level tablespoons walnuts or pine nuts
$\frac{1}{2}$ teaspoon salt, plus more as needed to taste
60 ml (2 fl oz) plus 2 tablespoons olive oil
100 ml (3 fl oz) plain yogurt
60 g (2 oz) firmly packed fresh basil leaves
250 g ($\frac{1}{2}$ lb) spaghettini
4 level teaspoons butter

1 Bring water to a boil in stockpot for pasta.
2 Fit food processor with metal blade. Drop garlic cloves through feed tube with machine running, and process until finely minced. (If using blender, mince garlic before putting it in container.) Add nuts salt, and 60 ml (2 fl oz) of the oil. Blend to a paste. Add yogurt and blend until smooth. Add basil and blend until smooth and evenly green. Adjust seasoning. Sauce should be slightly salty, or pasta will be bland.
3 Cover pesto sauce and let stand until ready to serve.
4 Add spaghettini to rapidly boiling water. Stir and cook, uncovered, until just tender – 7 to 9 minutes. Drain in colander, shaking well to remove excess water.
5 Add the remaining 2 tablespoons of the oil to empty stockpot. Add spaghettini and toss over low heat until lightly coated with oil.
6 To serve, divide spaghettini into 4 rimmed soup plates. Spoon $\frac{1}{4}$ of the pesto sauce over each portion and top each with 1 teaspoon butter.

Grilled Salmon Fillets with Chives in Lemon Butter Sauce

$1\frac{1}{2}$ tablespoons vegetable oil
500 to 625 g (1 to $1\frac{1}{4}$ lbs) skinless, boneless salmon
    fillets, cut into four equal portions
60 ml (2 fl oz) cold water
60 ml (2 fl oz) fresh lemon juice
$\frac{1}{2}$ teaspoon salt
175 g (6 oz) butter, softened and cut into small pieces

1 heaped tablespoon freshly snipped chives for garnish (optional)

1 Brush stove-top grill with 1 teaspoon of the oil and place grill over medium-high heat.
2 Rinse salmon fillets and pat dry. Remove any remaining bones with tweezers. Pound each fillet lightly to make all fillets of an even thickness. Brush tops of fillets liberally with oil.
3 Place salmon, oiled side down, on grill and cook until salmon begins to turn pale at edges and is well marked with grill ridges. Transfer with metal turner to oiled baking sheet, placing them marked side up. Set aside.
4 Heat oven to 190°C (375°F or Mark 5).
5 To prepare sauce, bring water, lemon juice, and salt to a boil in non-aluminium saucepan. Set saucepan over low heat and whisk in butter, a little at a time, allowing each batch of butter to be fully absorbed before adding more. When all butter is absorbed, remove saucepan from heat.
6 About 5 minutes before serving, place fish in oven. Bake just until tip of small sharp knife inserted into thickest part of fillet is hot when withdrawn.
7 Heat sauce until hot, but do not allow it to simmer. Divide sauce evenly among 4 heated dinner plates. Place piece of fish in centre of each plate. Garnish with chives, if desired.

Sliced Tomato and Goat Cheese Salad

350 g (³/₄ lb) ripe tomatoes
125 g (¹/₄ lb) log-type goat cheese
2 level tablespoons minced fresh parsley
60 ml (2 fl oz) red wine vinegar
Large pinch of salt (optional)
60 ml (2 fl oz) vegetable or safflower oil
60 ml (2 fl oz) olive oil
Freshly ground black pepper

1 With small paring knife, remove and discard cores from tomatoes. Cut tomatoes into 5 mm (¹/₄ inch) slices; then cut slices in half.
2 With wet knife, slice cheese into 2¹/₂ mm (¹/₈ inch) coins.
3 Alternate tomato and cheese slices on 4 salad plates. Place ¹/₂ tablespoon of the parsley down centre of each to form stripe, if desired, or sprinkle on. Set aside until ready to serve.
4 Place vinegar in jar. Add salt, if desired, oils, and

pepper. Cover tightly and set aside until ready to serve.
5 Just before serving, shake jar vigorously to mix vinaigrette. Pour dressing over tomato and cheese slices.

Added touch
For dessert, try a sampling of fresh fruits accompanied by hazelnut-butter cookies. You can find hazelnuts easily in any health food or speciality food shop. Before grinding the hazelnuts, toast them on a cookie sheet in a 150°C (300°F or Mark 2) oven, stirring them frequently to prevent burning. Let them cool completely. If you do not have a cookie press, put the dough on a long sheet of plastic wrap and form it into a 30 cm (12 inch) long roll, about 5 cm (2 inches) in diameter. Refrigerate the dough until it is thoroughly chilled, then slice it into 2¹/₂ cm (1 inch) rounds.

Hazelnut-Butter Cookies

125 g (4 oz) unsalted butter, softened to room temperature
100 g (3 oz) sugar
Pinch of salt
1 egg yolk
30 g (1 oz) ground toasted hazelnuts
125 g (4 oz) unbleached white flour

1 Put butter, sugar, and salt into large mixing bowl. Stir to combine. Add egg yolk and stir until thoroughly mixed.
2 Adjust oven rack to lowest position. Heat oven to 180°C (350°F or Mark 4).
3 Stir hazelnuts and flour into butter mixture, working until it comes together in a smooth mass. Transfer dough to cookie press fitted with large-opening design plate. Press out about 30 cookies on ungreased baking sheet. Bake 12 to 15 minutes, or until light brown ring forms around edges.
4 Remove cookies from sheet to cake rack to cool.

<table>
<tr><td>

Menu

2

</td><td>

Sliced Prosciutto with Country Bread
Pasta Salad with Asparagus and Shrimp

</td></tr>
</table>

Offer the prosciutto on bread as an appetizer. Meanwhile, you can put the finishing decorative touches on the pasta salad platter.

One of the easiest Italian summer appetizers is a platter of sliced prosciutto, which is cured, unsmoked ham. Select a top-quality ham, thinly sliced, that is deep pink, moist, and not too salty.

The colourful pasta salad with asparagus and red peppers is an appropriate late-spring or early summer meal. Instead of asparagus, you can use broccoli or snow peas. To make the shrimp go further, split medium-size shrimp lengthwise.

The cook suggests that you use only freshly roasted red peppers, which you can easily prepare yourself. If you have a gas stove, put the whole pepper directly on the flame. As the skin blackens, turn the pepper, roasting it until it is charred all over. After roasting, close the pepper in a bag to create steam and loosen the skin. Then rinse and rub off the blackened skins. If you have an electric cooker, put the peppers under the grill, turning them three or four times until charred. Scrape off the blackened skins and they are ready to use.

What to drink

Choose a crisp white Italian wine with some fruitiness: Lacryma Christi del Vesuvio, Pinot Bianco, or Verdicchio.

Start-to-Finish Steps

1 Follow prosciutto recipe.
2 Snap asparagus, clean shrimp, juice and zest lemon, and mince parsley and garlic for pasta recipe.
3 Follow pasta recipe steps 1 to 13. Serve with prosciutto and bread.

Sliced Prosciutto with Country Bread

250 g (½ lb) thinly sliced prosciutto
4 to 8 slices country-style bread
4 to 8 level tablespoons butter, slightly softened

Let prosciutto come to room temperature. Top slice of bread with chunk of butter and prosciutto.

Pasta Salad with Asparagus and Shrimp

24 slender asparagus spears, tough ends removed
250 g (½ lb) medium-size shrimp, peeled and
    deviened
1 large red bell pepper
125 g (4 oz) loosely packed pitted black olives
350 g (¾ lb) linguine
100 ml (3 fl oz) plus 3 tablespoons vegetable or
    safflower oil
1 teaspoon grated lemon zest
2½ tablespoons fresh lemon juice
2 cloves garlic, minced
2 teaspoons Dijon mustard
2 level tablespoons freshly minced parsley
¼ teaspoon salt
Freshly ground black pepper
60 ml (2 fl oz) olive oil

1   Put water in vegetable steamer to fill space below steamer basket.
2   Cut asparagus about ⅔ way down from tips. Place tips in steamer basket. Place basket in pot, cover, and set over high heat.
3   Cut remaining ⅓ of asparagus stalks at an angle into 1 cm (½ inch) slices. Add to steamer basket. Steam until tips are barely resistant when pierced with tip of small sharp knife, about 5 to 6 minutes. Remove basket but do not discard liquid. Spread asparagus on kitchen towel to cool.
4   Return steaming liquid to a boil. Remove from heat, add shrimp, stir, cover, and let stand until shrimp are curled, but still tender – about 3 to 5 minutes. With slotted spoon, transfer shrimp to kitchen towel. Cool, then split each shrimp lengthwise.
5   Transfer 3 tablespoons of the steaming liquid to small bowl. Freeze the remaining liquid for use as stock, or discard.
6   Bring water to a boil in stockpot for pasta.
7   Char red pepper on top of gas range or under high grill, turning frequently until pepper is blackened. Transfer to paper bag.
8   Drain olives and slice each in half.
9   Scrape charred skin from red pepper. Core and seed red pepper. Open pepper flat and slice into julienne strips. Set aside.
10 Add linguine to boiling water. Stir well and cook at a rolling boil, uncovered, until just tender, about 6 to 9 minutes. Drain in colander, then rinse thoroughly under cold water to cool. Shake very well to remove excess liquid. Transfer pasta to large bowl and toss with 3 tablespoons of the vegetable oil. Spread out pasta, tossing occasionally to prevent sticking.
11 Whisk lemon zest, juice, garlic, mustard, parsley, salt, and pepper into 3 tablespoons of reserved liquid. Slowly whisk in olive oil and the remaining vegetable oil to form smooth, emulsified sauce. Add salt and pepper to taste.
12 Add pasta sauce to cooled pasta. Add sliced asparagus pieces, olives, and shrimp. Toss thoroughly. Adjust seasoning.
13 Arrange asparagus tips and red pepper strips on each plate, alternating them like spokes of wheel. Centre large swirl of pasta salad over tips, allowing buds to show.

Added touch

This simple dessert calls for fresh raspberries, a rarity in most markets. If you cannot find them, substitute whole frozen raspberries, or any other fresh berry – such as blueberries, strawberries, or blackberries.

Raspberries with Custard Sauce

500 g (1 lb) raspberries, washed and drained

The sauce:
6 egg yolks from large eggs
250 ml (8 fl oz) milk
250 ml (8 fl oz) half-and-half milk and cream
100 g (3 oz) sugar
1 to 1¼ teaspoons vanilla extract
Brandy, framboise, or kirsch to taste (optional)

1   Place yolks and milk in 2½ ltr (4 pt) saucepan. Whisk to mix thoroughly.
2   In separate saucepan, heat half-and-half with sugar, stirring well, over low heat just until sugar dissolves. Mixture can be scalded, but do not boil.
3   Strain about 125 ml (4 fl oz) of the hot sugar mixture into yolks, stirring. Put saucepan with yolks over low heat, and gradually add the remaining sugar mixture. Stir constantly until mixture thickens to consistency of unbeaten whipping cream, about 10 to 15 minutes. Remove from heat.
4   Strain custard sauce into bowl. If desired, set bowl over ice for rapid cooling. When cool, stir in vanilla and liqueur to taste. Cover and refigerate until chilled.

<table>
<tr><td>

Menu

3

</td><td>

Pasta and Mussels with Herbed Tomato-and-Garlic Sauce
Quick Curry-Roasted Chicken
Mushroom, Endive, and Watercress Salad
with Italian Vinaigrete

</td></tr>
</table>

The pasta recipe in this menu – a light seafood pasta that you serve in soup bowls – calls for mussels, a shellfish generally available year round. After you have cleaned the mussels, check carefully for any that are open; discard these at once for this is a sure sign that they are no longer alive or fresh. After steaming them, again check the mussels, discarding any that have *not* opened; these are not fresh either. If your market does not carry mussels, you can substitute

Present the pasta with mussels on a large platter, then serve it into heated rimmed soup plates at the table. A bed of curly parsley contrasts well with the golden curry-roasted chicken and unites it visually with the other two dishes.

quickly steamed fresh scallops, shrimp, sliced squid, or lobster-tail meat. Time your cooking so that this appetizer course is ready to serve and eat about 15 minutes before the chicken finishes roasting.

To give the chicken a rosier hue, Jane Salzfass Freiman sprinkles it with a light dusting of medium-strength or hot chili powder just after rubbing it with the curry paste.

The mushroom, endive, and watercress salad is dressed with a rich Italian vinaigrette. Its principal ingredient is balsamic vinegar, an aged dark vinegar made only in Modena, Italy. It has a rich aroma and its taste – pungent yet sweet-sour – enhances strong flavourful foods and salad greens. If you cannot find

this special vinegar, which is available in speciality food stores and some quality supermarkets, use a dark red wine vinegar instead.

What to drink

To accompany this menu, which offers several distinctive herbs and spices, pick a mild white wine that will not detract from the cooking – a good Soave, for example – or serve a spicy, fruity wine that can share the spotlight: a dry California or Alsatian Gewurztraminer.

Start-to-Finish Steps

1 Follow chicken recipe steps 1 to 4. While chicken roasts, continue steps below.
2 Follow pasta recipe steps 1 to 4.
3 Follow vinaigrette recipe.
4 Remove watercress stem for salad recipe and follow salad recipe steps 1 to 5.
5 Follow pasta recipe steps 5 to 10.
6 Follow chicken recipe step 5, salad recipe step 6, and pasta recipe step 11. Serve.

Pasta and Mussels with Herbed Tomato-and-Garlic Sauce

2 tablespoons dried basil
1 teaspoon dried thyme
1 teaspoon dried sage
2 teaspoons dried marjoram
2 teaspoons dried summer savory
500 g (1 lb) fresh mussels
2 cloves garlic
125 ml (4 fl oz) water
125 ml (4 fl oz) dry white wine
2 large tomatoes (about 350 g (¾ lb))
60 ml (2 fl oz) olive oil
3 level tablespoons tomato paste
250 g (½ lb) medium-size tubular pasta
15 g (½ oz) minced fresh parsley
Salt
Freshly ground black pepper

1 Combine basil, thyme, sage, marjoram, and summer savory in small jar.
2 Soak mussels in basin of cold salted water.

3 Bring water to a boil in stockpot for pasta.

4 Mince garlic very fine and place it in non-aluminium skillet. Set aside.

5 Brush each mussel to clean away dirt, and remove mussels' fibres by pulling them free of shell. Rinse mussels well under cold running water and place in saucepan. Add water and wine; cover and bring to a boil, then continue to cook until mussels open. Transfer them to bowl to cool, discarding those that remain closed or only slightly open. Pour steaming liquid through strainer lined with paper towel or coffee filter; reserve liquid.

6 Dip tomatoes in hot water from stockpot about 15 seconds to loosen skins. Peel, seed, and coarsely chop tomatoes.

7 Add olive oil to skillet with garlic. Cook over low heat about 1 minute, just until fragrant. Add tomatoes, strained mussel broth, and tomato paste. Add any liquid that has accumulated in bowl with mussels by pouring it through strainer lined with paper towel. Stir well, then simmer rapidly 12 to 15 minutes, until mixture reduces by half and forms thick sauce measuring 250-350 ml (8-12 fl oz).

8 Pull mussels from shells. Discard shells.

9 Add pasta to boiling water. Stir well and cook at a rolling boil, uncovered, until just tender, usually 7 to 9 minutes. Drain in colander.

10 Reheat tomato sauce while pasta drains. Stir in parsley, salt, pepper, and 1 teaspoon of the mixed dried herbs.

11 Add drained pasta to skillet with sauce and toss over low heat. Add mussels and mix thoroughly. Adjust seasoning from the remaining mixed dried herbs (storing any leftover herbs for use in other, similar recipes), and serve in heated rimmed soup bowls.

Quick Curry-Roasted Chicken

1¹/₄ to 1¹/₂ kg (2¹/₂ to 3 lb) frying chicken
¹/₄ teaspoon curry powder
Large pinch of salt (optional)
1 tablespoon olive oil
Freshly ground black pepper

1 Heat oven between 220° and 230°C (425° and 450°F or Mark 7-8).

2 Lay chicken with its breast side down, and cut down centre of tail. Continue cutting through backbone and to one side of remaining neck bone. Open chicken flat by grasping two cut sides and pushing down. Remove fat and glands, especially under neck skin. Pat chicken dry with paper towels. Turn breast side up and flatten with heel of your hand. Cut off wing tips.

3 Put curry powder and salt into small bowl. Rub chicken, inside and out, with half of the oil. Make paste of curry, salt, and remaining oil, and rub on both sides of chicken to season it. Sprinkle lightly with salt, if desired, and pepper.

4 Transfer chicken to shallow metal roasting pan, skin side up. Tuck wings under. Add neck and giblets, if desired; reserve liver for another use. Roast until leg joint moves freely and skin is golden, about 50 to 55 minutes.

5 Cut into quarters to serve.

Mushroom, Endive, and Watercress Salad

1 large bunch watercress, stems removed
250 g (¹/₂ lb) Belgian Endive
125 g (¹/₄ lb) fresh mushrooms (about 6 medium-size)
Italian vinaigrette (see following recipe)

1 Place watercress in medium-size bowl of cold water.

2 Remove and discard stem end of endive. Add endive to water.

3 Wipe mushrooms clean with damp cloth. Slice medium thick and place in salad bowl.

4 Drain endive. Shake endive to dry, and cut crosswise into 3 sections. Roll up in part of dry cloth towel.

5 Drain watercress and spin dry. Roll in remainder of the towel. Put in refrigerator 5 minutes, then unroll and add to salad bowl. Refrigerate until ready to serve.

6 For serving, whisk Italian vinaigrette well and toss with greens.

Italian Vinaigrette

2 tablespoons balsamic vinegar
Pinch of salt (optional)
¹/₄ teaspoon Dijon mustard
3 tablespoons olive oil
3 tablespoons vegetable oil
Freshly ground black pepper

With small whisk, mix vinegar, salt, if desired, and mustard in small bowl. Slowly whisk in oils to form thickened dressing. Whisk in pepper.

Meet the Cooks

Helen Witty

Helen Witty lives in New York. She has written about food and related subjects for many magazines, including *Gourmet*, *Food & Wine* and *Family Circle*. A senior editor of *The Cook's Catalogue*, Helen Witty is also a co-author.

Alfredo Viazzi

A native of Savona, Italy, Alfredo Viazzi is the owner and executive chef of several Italian restaurants in New York City's Greenwich Village. Also an author, his approach to cooking is based on the love of food, improvisation, and a sense of theatre.

Ed Giobbi

Ed Giobbi is a painter of international reputation as well as a talented cook specializing in Italian food. He frequently travels to Italy and expounds the joys of Italian regional food in his book, *Italian Family Cooking*.

Bernice Hunt

Although she is not a professional chef, Bernice Hunt is an ardent amateur cook. She has travelled extensively throughout Italy and has become a convert to northern Italian cuisine— which inspires her own cooking style. Bernice Hunt is also the author of two cookery books.

Sylvia Rosenthal

Sylvia Rosenthal has been involved in the business of good eating and good cooking for all of her adult life. Always interested in nutrition, she published her first book in 1962, *Live High on Low Fat*.

Diane Darrow and Tom Maresca

Diane Darrow and her husband, Tom Maresca, live and work in New York City and cook mostly in the Italian manner. Diane Darrow has taught wine appreciation classes, and Tom Maresca is the wine consultant for the *Great Meals in Minutes* series. Together, they have published numerous articles on food, wine, dining, and travel, as well as pursued their separate careers as editor and teacher.

Jane Salzfass Freiman

Jane Salzfass Freiman, a Chicago-based cookery instructor for several years, holds a diploma in French culinary arts from Luberon College, in Avignon, France. She has travelled extensively in Italy and is a specialist in Italian cooking. A food writer, she is the author of *The Art of Food Processor Cooking*.

A Wealth of Herbs

Increasingly, herbs are arriving in the markets fresh; the proliferation of health stores and other specialíst shops has widened choice, and many cooks with gardens have taken to raising their own. Recent ethnic influences have called attention to once seemingly esoteric herbs. Coriander, for one, is at last gaining deserved popularity in Europe, although cooks in Asia and the Middle East have been using it for centuries.

Anyone wishing to dry fresh herbs can tie them loosely in a bundle and hang them upside down in a cool, dark, well-ventilated place for several weeks. When the leaves are completely dried, strip them from the stems and store them in an airtight container.

Two swifter methods of preserving herbs make use of the microwave oven and the freezer. To microwave herbs, place five or six sprigs at a time between paper towels and microwave them on high for 1 to 3 minutes until the leaves are brittle. Store the leaves loosely in airtight jars.

To freeze herbs, rinse the sprigs and pat them dry. Strip the leaves off the stems and put them into a heavy-duty plastic bag. Gently flatten the bag to force out the air, seal the bag tightly, and place it in your freezer. Use the leaves as the need arises.

Basil (also called sweet basil): This fragrant herb, with its underlying flavour of anise and hint of clove, goes particularly well with tomato.

Chervil: The small, lacy leaves of this herb have a taste akin to parsley with a touch of anise. It is good in salads and salad dressings. Chervil is popular in France where it is often an ingredient in herb mixtures, including *fines herbes*. When used in cooking, chervil should be added at the end, lest its subtle flavour be lost.

Chives: The smallest of the onions, chives grow in grassy clumps. When finely cut, the hollow leaves contribute their delicate, oniony flavour to fresh salads and raw vegetables. Chives should always be used fresh, as dried ones are virtually tasteless.

Coriander (also called cilantro): The serrated leaves of the coriander plant impart a distinctive fragrance and a flavour that is both mildly sweet and bitter. Coriander leaves should be used fresh or added at the end of cooking if their flavour is to be appreciated fully.

Dill: A sprightly herb with feathery leaves, dill enhances cucumber and many other fresh vegetables, as well as fish and shellfish. When used in cooking, dill should be added towards the end of the process to preserve its delicate flavour. Both dill seeds and dill leaves can be